FROM STRENGTH TO STRENGTH
Lectures from Shearith Israel

FROM STRENGTH TO STRENGTH
Lectures from Shearith Israel

Edited by

Rabbi Marc D. Angel

Published for
Congregation Shearith Israel
by
Sepher-Hermon Press, Inc.

FROM STRENGTH TO STRENGTH
Lectures from Shearith Israel
Copyright © 1998 Marc D. Angel
Published by
Sepher-Hermon Press, Inc.
1265 46th Street, Brooklyn, NY 11219

ISBN 0-87203-152-7

Library of Congress Cataloging-in-Publication Data
From Strength to Strength: Lectures from Shearith Israel / edited by
    Marc D. Angel.
        p.   cm.
    Includes bibliographical references.
    ISBN 0-87203-152-7
    1. Congregation Shearith Israel (New York, N.Y.) 2. Sephardim - New
York (State) - New York - History. 3. Jews - New York (State) - New York
- History. 4. Judaism. I. Angel, Marc. II. Congregation Shearith Israel
(New York, N.Y.)
F128.9.J576 1998   97-50455
909'.04924--dc21   CIP

CONTENTS

V

INTRODUCTION

Congregation Shearith Israel has been providing Jewish education for our community for nearly three hundred and fifty years. One of its central purposes has always been to disseminate the teachings of Judaism in a comprehensible and meaningful way. The synagogue continues to serve not only as a place of prayer and communal gathering, but also as a place of Torah study.

Over the years, many thousands of people have participated in the educational programs at Shearith Israel. Through the generous education fund established by Jack and Susan Rudin, we have been able to offer a wide variety of classes, public lectures, seminars and cultural programs.

This book, published with the support of the Jack and Susan Rudin Education Fund, provides the texts of a number of lectures which have been given at Shearith Israel during the past several years. The first section includes lectures dealing with the specific history and culture of Congregation Shearith Israel, the oldest Jewish congregation in North America. These lectures were delivered as part of the centennial celebration of our Sisterhood, as well as the centennial celebration of our current synagogue building on Seventieth Street and Central Park West. The second section of the book includes papers by leading thinkers and scholars on a range of themes.

Through the publication of this book, the Shearith Israel Education Program is enabled to reach many who were unable to attend the lectures in person. In the past, the Congregation has published, from time to time, individual lectures and programs given at Shearith Israel. This is the first time that we are issuing an entire volume, and we are hopeful that it will meet with an enthusiastic reception from its readers.

I express sincere thanks to the authors who have contributed articles for this book, as well as to Mr. Samuel Gross of Sepher-Hermon Press who has published the volume for us with his customary devotion and skill. I thank Mrs. Hennie Imberman for her devoted work in preparing the manuscript for publication.

Last but not least, I thank the members of the Congregation and community who have participated actively in our educational programs. To the Board of Trustees of Congregation Shearith Israel, and to all who have been supportive of the educational programs sponsored by the Congregation, I express my gratitude and appreciation.

SECTION ONE

TRADITION AND CHANGE: CELEBRATING ONE HUNDRED YEARS OF SISTERHOOD*

DECEMBER 9, 1996

by Judith S. Kaye

As a person who loves celebrations, this is for me a triple treat. Tonight, we celebrate Hanukkah; we celebrate the 100th anniversary of the Sisterhood; and we celebrate the life of Alice Davis Menken.

Celebrations are certainly fun, but often they are also much more significant. With the cycle of commemoration, we take a moment to reflect on great achievements of the past. At the same time, we set benchmarks that allow us to measure how far we've come both as a people and individually in our own lives. And then we move forward into the future, enriched and inspired by the example of those who have gone before us.

Tonight's first celebration-Hanukkah-of course commemorates the faith and courage of the Maccabees, who overcame superior forces to recapture the Temple in Jerusalem and re-establish the freedom of religious worship that Antiochus had taken from them.

---

*Two superb Susans were central to the research for, and preparation of, this essay: Susan Knipps, my Counsel and Susan Tobin, the Congregation's archivist.

1

Hanukkah also celebrates the miracle of the precious bit of oil that burned wondrously for a full eight days in the rededicated Temple. That shows how with faith and commitment, we can achieve more than anyone would think possible. It shows that a single spark can ignite a process that continues on and on against all odds. Indeed, at Hanukkah, each night we light one additional candle, symbolizing not simply the miracle of survival but even more astoundingly, a miracle of increasing strength and growing vibrancy.

It is intriguing that, although women are bound to perform few of the mitzvot tied to particular times of the day, they have the same obligation as men to light the Hanukkah candles. Some say this is because women were part of the miracle, some say that it is because the miracle actually happened through women. Whatever the reason, it makes this an especially appropriate occasion for our second celebration, the centennial of the Sisterhood.

With the Sisterhood centennial, we also commemorate a story of faith and commitment, of women united together who went out into the world and accomplished more than anyone thought possible, a group that has not only survived but also grown stronger with time. From its earliest relief work on the Lower East Side, to its work on behalf of refugees from the horrors of Europe, to the many projects of today - Bible classes, work for the Succah and for the Sanctuary, help for hospitals and the needy, support for Nahlat Dalton (the Israeli community established in honor of Dr. and Mrs. Pool) - the Sisterhood has kept the flame of faith and commitment burning brightly for one hundred years.

Our third reason for celebration tonight is Alice Davis Menken, Sisterhood president from 1900 to 1929. Even by today's standards, this was a most extraordinary woman.

To appreciate how truly amazing Alice Menken's accomplishments were in their time, we have to step back one hundred years to 1896. Of course, we wouldn't be stepping back in this building - it was almost, but not quite, completed. Instead, we'd be gathered in Shearith Israel's fourth home, on Nineteenth Street, having arrived there by horse-drawn buses, cable cars or steam-powered elevated trains. Thankfully, we would have electric street lighting in the neighborhood. By 1896, electric street lights hadn't reached "the Dakotas" of Central Park West, but they had been extended all the way up to 42nd Street.

The turn of the century was a time of enormous turmoil in New York City, with hundreds of thousands of immigrants streaming into our harbor, many crowding into tenements and sweatshops, seeking a new life in a new world. Physical conditions were harsh, as were social conditions, especially for women. If this really were 1896, there wouldn't have been a single female judge to honor - even the doors of all the law schools throughout New York State were closed to women until 1890.

Women back then faced discrimination in almost every aspect of their lives. They were denied the right to vote, and while they had by then made progress in the right to own property, they still had to deal with the prevailng societal attitude that they were themselves the property of their fathers or husbands. For women, to "have opinions and to voice them was not regarded as good form even in the home." (Irving Howe, *World of our Fathers,* p. 265 [1976]). New York one hundred years ago was thus a daunting place for women who wanted to venture beyond the familial threshold.

And that is exactly the world in which Alice Menken-a great granddaughter of Hazzan Moses Levi Maduro Peixotto, herself steeped in Sephardic tradition-rolled up her sleeves and went to work. Led by a faith that did not stop at the synagogue door, Alice Menken went out to help those who had been dealt a much harsher hand in life.

She organized clubs and religious classes for young people on the Lower East Side. She was instrumental in the founding of the Sisterhood's settlement houses. She was a pioneer in social work for women caught up in the criminal justice system. Alice Menken worked in the field, not in an Ivory Tower. "After a full day's work she would go late at night to the Night Court for Women, sit with the poor victims dragged in by the police, sustain them in their difficulties at court, and [then] follow through with their problems and those of their family." (David and Tamar de Sola Pool, *An Old Faith in the New World*, p. 375 [1955]).

One can only wonder what Hazzan Peixotto would have thought about his great granddaughter as she sat up night after night with prostitutes brought in by the vice squad. I would hope that he would have been proud, for this work was the natural extension of Alice Menken's abiding religious faith. In the words of Dr. Pool, "Her religion was not limited to the forms of the ritual which she loved, but was an outward example to those who may doubt the value of religion." ("Associates Mourn Mrs. M. M. Menken," The New York Times, March 16, 1936).

A theme that emerges from a review of the work of Alice Menken and the Sisterhood is the struggle to balance the issues of tradition and change in a world where change is constant. It is clear that in the Sisterhood's work with the so-called "Oriental Jews"-meaning Jews from Turkey, the Balkans, Greece and Syria-one goal was to "Americanize" them by teaching them English and introducing them to the principles and institutions of this country. A wonderful example was a Fourth of July celebration in 1912 where the Sisterhood distributed five hundred copies of the Declaration of Independence-translated into Ladino.

But as they worked at assimilation, the women of the Sisterhood were careful to preserve the distinct rituals and traditions brought to these shores by our newest Americans. Change, yes, but preserve the fundamentals.

For courts and judges today, balancing tradition and change continues to be the greatest challenge of all. The courts are a branch of government steeped in tradition. Judges wear robes of a different era; clerks call a courtroom to order with words used for generations; the architecture of our courthouses reflects designs of the past. These tangible signs of continuity serve to reinforce the intangible concept of stability in the law itself.

Courts honor and preserve the past, but law exists to function in the present. Every day, the disputes before us involve breath-taking new technologies, perplexing new social problems, undreamed-of new family arrangements. Sometimes the established rules are adequate to decide the matter; sometimes completely new answers must be found. As in so many important areas of our lives, for guidance always courts and judges must look to the core principles and central values that define us — justice, fairness, respect for each individual's inherent worth and dignity. Change, yes, but preserve the fundamentals.

Judges are not the only ones who face this vexing issue of

balancing change and tradition. We all do today - women especially. Thankfully, the choices we face are not as stark as those Alice Menken confronted. Today we see the acceptance of women as equals, as full human beings capable of limitless achievement. Today women enjoy a right to have strong opinions and to voice them both within and outside the home. Even the word "Sisterhood" has taken on radically new meaning as a symbol of change wrought by the women's movement.

One recent sign of change for women was the brand new, first-time phenomenon in national politics this year - the "Soccer Mom." As *The New York Times* reported, "The hands that steered the minivan were also deciding whether to turn left or right in the presidential election." Instead of a political banner, the Soccer Mom wears a button with the picture of her daughter, a halfback on the team. The Soccer Mom has a laptop computer, a cell phone and a beeper but she also cares very deeply about America's core values. She wants good schools, safe streets, a strong economy, more opportunity, a better life for her family and yours. Change, yes-absolutely yes-but preserve the fundamentals. And as you know, this was indeed The Year of the Soccer Mom, who proved herself a key political constituency.

Thinking about Alice Menken, about the Sisterhood centennial and about Hanukkah, I have come to see tonight as a celebration of the "Torah Mom." The phrase, by the way, includes daughters as well as mothers. The "Torah Mom" also centers her life around core traditional values. But like Alice Menken, the "Torah Mom" does not see these values as in any way restricting, confining or impeding her as a full person. To the contrary, she sees her religious faith as a positive force that enables her to be her own person, to enjoy miracles and to go out and make miracles.

Tonight I am delighted to receive this award, particularly because it comes from treasured friends and fellow congregants with whom Stephen and I, our children and now our grandchildren, have shared so many life milestones. I thank Ruth Blumberg and the Sisterhood especially for introducing me to one of our Founding Mothers, Alice Davis Menken, who surely deserves a prominent place among Shearith Israel's most outstanding figures.

This evening inaugurates a year-long celebration, The Year of the Torah Mom, honoring all the extraordinary women of this Congregation. I suspect, and hope, that as the year unfolds, we will have many opportunities to explore their faith, their commitment, their achievements, their challenges and their successes in balancing tradition and change, as we together write the history that will be reviewed at the next centennial celebration.

In the meanwhile, Happy Hanukkah, Happy Centennial and a Happy Next Hundred Years of Sisterhood.

A CENTENNIAL OF SERVICE*

SOCIAL ACTIVISM AND THE SISTERHOOD OF THE

SPANISH AND PORTUGUESE SYNAGOGUE

by Fortuna Calvo-Roth

"As a people, we are of course defined by our history. As Jews and as members of this Congregation, it therefore is entirely fitting that we study our distinctive past and take pride in the outstanding contributions of one of our own." (Chief Judge Judith S. Kaye, excerpted from a talk she gave in appreciation of Supreme Court Justice Benjamin Nathan Cardozo, delivered at Congregation Shearith Israel in May 1995.)

Tomorrow, [December 9, 1996,] during a special ceremony of thanksgiving marking the 100th anniversary of the Sisterhood of the Spanish and Portuguese Synagogue, the Honorable Judith S. Kaye, Chief Judge of the State of New York and of its Court of Appeals, will receive the Alice Davis Menken Award. Established this year, the award was created to commemorate the Sisterhood Centennial in its year-long celebration and to honor the pioneering spirit and

---

*Parts of this text, based on research by Susan Tobin, archivist of Congregation Shearith Israel, were used in an address to the Jewish Historical Society of New York on December 8, 1996.

achievements of the women of its Congregation. Judge Kaye has been a member of the Congregation for the past three decades.

The Spanish and Portuguese Synagogue, Congregation Shearith Israel, located for the last century at 70th Street and Central Park West, was founded in 1654. It was the first Jewish congregation established in North America, and remains the oldest continuing Congregation to date. Involved with charitable work since its founding and being the only Jewish congregation in New York City until 1825, it was up to that time the only such institution to cater to the needs of the city's Jewish population.

Women's organized involvement began in 1820 with the establishment of the Female Hebrew Benevolent Society, which became consolidated with the men's Hebrew Relief Society in 1870. A decade later, poet and essayist Emma Lazarus, famous for the lines of "The New Colossus" engraved on the pedestal of the Statue of Liberty, and a member of the Congregation, became involved in helping new immigrants settle in this country. At that time, and until the 1920s, when it was recognized as a profession, social work was the domain of volunteers.

In 1896, The Shearith Israel Sisterhood was established "to do philanthropic and educational work by personal service and other practicable methods." It worked with other Sisterhoods under the auspices of the United Hebrew Charities to help immigrants on the Lower East Side of Manhattan. The name was changed to "Sisterhood of the Spanish and Portuguese Synagogue".

Many of the women of the Congregation have stood at the forefront of social and educational institutions, and served as defenders of civil and religious freedoms for Jews and non-Jews alike. Some of the early names are those of Alice Davis Menken, Annie Nathan Meyer, Frances Nathan Wolff and Maud Nathan. More recently, the names of Lillian Henry Hendricks, Tamar de Sola Pool and Chief Judge Kaye stand out.

The Alice Davis Menken Award honors the memory of the woman who served as president of the Sisterhood from 1900 to 1929. A pioneer in the field of social welfare and the court system, she is the author of "On the Side of Mercy: Problems in Social Readjustment" and became the first female prison trustee in New York.

Under her leadership, the Sisterhood made valuable contributions to the social issues of the time:

- It assisted in the settlement of thousands of immigrants from Czarist Russia and from the disintegrating Ottoman Empire.
- Sisterhood Probation Committee members* were often in Night Court to help in the rehabilitation of young women on parole.
- The "Neighborhood Care" program accounted for more than 300 visits to families in need, assisting them with basic necessities like coal, clothing, food, employment and medical care at home or at the hospital as well as summer outings.
- Members sustained and did volunteer work in schools which counteracted the work of Christian missionaries

*The Federation for the Support of Jewish Philanthropic Societies took over the probation work in 1919, coordinating preventive and rescue work for Jewish juvenile and adult delinquents in a central committee.

on Manhattan's Lower East Side. While supporting the acculturation process, including the study of English, they were equally intent on maintaining Jewish identity.

In an article published in March 1934 in the "Women's League Outlook," Maud Nathan, the Sisterhood's first president, wrote: "Whenever I hear Jews spoken of as aliens, and Gentiles spoken of as Americans, I marvel at the ignorance of people who are supposed to be cultured and well-informed." Like her parents and her husband, she attended Shearith Israel and she was active in the New York section of the National Council of Jewish Women.

Maud Nathan was Sisterhood president from 1896 to 1897, shortly after the death of her daughter. The New York Exchange for Women's Work and the Women's Auxiliary of the Civil Service Reform Association recruited her not only for her social position but also perhaps because she represented the growing Jewish community. More importantly, she was president of the New York Consumers' League. Today, however, she is best remembered as a prominent suffragist.

During the fight for women's suffrage, she took part in 24-hour speech marathons from automobiles around the city. Once, she was heckled by a man who shouted, "It's all very well for you to vote, Mrs. Nathan, but how would you like your cook to vote?" To which she replied, "He does."

On another occasion, she asked recent immigrants to acknowledge their obligation to justice, even if they had to sacrifice some of their "Oriental customs."

Some of these customs were typical of traditional societies. For example, Sephardic Jews from the Middle East were prone to stay at home and not become social activists. Also, Middle

Eastern Jews did not speak English, Yiddish or German. Most spoke Judeo-Spanish, Greek or Arabic. Even those from Turkey who shared a common language mixed mainly with their own kind. They would frequent cafés in the Lower East Side, each one specializing in clients from specific towns. My own father settled on Christie St. in 1913, in the area where the Sisterhood's Neighborhood House was established.

His arrival in lower Manhattan typifies the achievements of social activism. At the gangplank, he was met by a representative of la Sociedad, as he called the Federation of Jewish Charities, and he answered with a resounding "yes" to all four questions: Are you Jewish? Are you Sephardic? Do you need a place to stay? Do you want a job? The next day at dawn he left his new abode for a new job and the start of a new life, far from his besieged hometown of Edirne, a Turkish town invaded by bordering Bulgaria.

My own arrival in New York, four decades later, echoes his, but with a twist: At the time of the Sinai War and Suez crisis of 1956, I was hired by the Israeli government in Mexico to work for two months in New York, at the Mission of Israel to the United Nations. Like my father, I was met at my port of entry (Idlewild,) whisked off to my new abode and taken the next morning to my new job and the beginning of a new life. But while my father left New York after a three-year stay, New York became my true hometown - more so than Paris, where I was born, or Lima, where I was raised. Maybe I was influenced by his glowing memories of this city.

Despite these differences, the new Sephardic immigrants had more in common with Shearith Israel and its Sisterhood than with anyone else in New York. The Sisterhood's priority was to promote a "spirit of confidence in and kinship with us."

In fact, home life was also a priority for Sisterhood leaders. In her memoir, "My Life and Memories of New York Over Eighty Years," Sisterhood vice president Frances Nathan Wolff modestly recalls:

"When my children reached an age when I felt that I could, without neglecting them, undertake some charitable work, I commenced visiting several families on the Lower East Side. (...) I recall one family that lived in a cellar in the rear of a tenement where the rays of the sun never penetrated. Of course, that was before the Federation of Jewish Charities had been established and now trained workers accomplish much more than an amateur did in my day."

Under Sisterhood auspices, Mrs. Wolff formed two clubs for young people of different ages. There were dancing classes, debates, dramatics, athletics and music, and entertainments at Hanukkah and Purim. Both eventually became part of the Sisterhood. She also was an active member of the Succoth, Sewing Circle, Finance and Cultural Society of the Sisterhood as well as a member of the House Committee of the Synagogue and vice chairman of the Holy Vestment Committee.

"In 1930--she writes--in conjunction with the Red Cross, the Sisterhood of the Spanish and Portuguese Synagogue was able to obtain unmade garments for women and children free of charge. I asked a number of my friends to meet in my apartment twice a week to make the garments and during the winter months one thousand and thirty five garments were finished. Half of these were sent to the Red Cross and the other half were distributed among many different Jewish organizations through the Sisterhood."

In addition, she chaired the Youth Aliyah of Hadassah and

the annual fundraising drive for Federation of Jewish Charities.

By contrast, Annie Nathan Meyer, who was Maud's sister and Frances' cousin, is best known as an antisuffrage feminist and a founder and trustee (1893-1942) of Barnard College.

Mainly self-educated, Mrs. Meyer decided to find independent funding for a women's college affiliated with Columbia and persuaded 50 prominent New Yorkers to sign a memorial to the trustees. In an article in The Nation (1888), she appealed to civic pride to promote the idea of a women's college with high academic standards. Besides recruiting Barnard's first board of trustees and signing the lease for the college's first building, she claimed to have pointed out almost all of the initial contributors. She was acutely interested in maintaining a Jewish presence at Barnard, protecting Jewish students against slights, and making sure they represented the type of Jewish woman she considered suitable.

Lillian Henry Hendricks is another woman whose family has been closely identified with New York City Jewry, and in particular the Spanish and Portuguese Synagogue. Mrs. Hendricks served as chairman of the Sisterhood's nursery committee, and she was elected Sisterhood treasurer and first vice president. She was also a director of the Columbia Religious and Industrial School for Girls, and during the Second World War, actively served the American Red Cross. Her daughter, Rosalie Nathan Hendricks, was a Sisterhood board member for more than 25 years and her granddaughter, Ruth Hendricks Schulson, was Sisterhood president for eight years. Their work adds up to 100 years of involvement in the Sisterhood.

Besides Ruth Schulson, whom I was delighted to nominate as Sisterhood president, I had great pleasure in knowing the remarkable Tamar de Sola Pool, wife of Congregation Shearith Israel's Rabbi David de Sola Pool. She was an ardent Zionist leader and a co-founder of Youth Aliyah. A graduate of what is now Hunter College, Mrs. Pool won an international travel scholarship for postgraduate studies at the University of Paris, and later taught French, Latin and Greek at Hunter College.

She met Dr. Pool at a Young Judea meeting, of which he was president, and they were married the following year at Shearith Israel, where he was assistant minister.

After her marriage, Mrs. Pool worked as a Sisterhood board member but is better recognized in the United States and in Israel for her work with Hadassah. She was Chair of the Hebrew University-Hadassah Medical School Building Fund campaign, editor of the Hadassah newsletter, president of its New York Chapter and of National Hadassah. She was also given the title of honorary president of Hadassah. From 1934 on, through Youth Aliyah, she sought to rescue Jewish children from Nazi persecution, resettling them in what is now Israel. In the spring of 1947 she had the opportunity to visit the detention camps in Cyprus, but if she went she would be unable to return to New York in time for Passover. She sent a cable home: should she go to Cyprus, she asked her husband, or should she come home? The reply consisted of one word: "Cyprus." Mrs. Pool worked until almost the end of a life that spanned more than nine decades. Born in Jerusalem and raised in Hoboken, N.J., she was also active in the National Council of Jewish Women and the World Zionist Organization. She wrote a biography of Henrietta Szold, the founder of Hadassah, co-authored with Dr. Pool a history of the congregation, "An Old Faith in the New World, Portrait of Shearith Israel, 1654-1954," and "Is There an Answer? An

Inquiry into Some Human Dilemmas."

She spoke to me often about Eliezer Ben Yehudah's work to reinstate Hebrew as a spoken language and gave a lecture on this subject when she was about 90 years old at the Ninth World Congress of Sociology at Uppsala University in Sweden. At the time of her death she was working on a biography of her husband. My personal memories are the keen interest she took in my children, and a particular telephone call requesting a copy of the speech my daughter Carla gave at her Confirmation (now Bat-Mitzvah) ceremony.

I became involved with the Sisterhood in 1980 and served as program chair and first vice president for several years before becoming co-president for one year. We had the Sewing Circle, which is now the "Tuesday-do-Something" group chaired by Ruth Schulson. Other traditions which continue are the Theater Party, book reviews and lectures by invited speakers on current issues.

But while the structure remains, there is no doubt that the Sisterhood is experiencing a crisis common to a majority of women's volunteer organizations. The higher cost of living coupled with the desire and/or need to form part of the workplace and to carve out careers is felt in the decreasing number of active younger board members and a marked lessening of social activism.

When the Sisterhood's impressive contribution to social welfare gave way to the era of the professional social worker, its members adapted to change and turned to an area where their efforts were sorely needed: fundraising. And fundraising they successfully did for many decades.

Many years ago, there were elaborate balls at the Waldorf

Astoria, elegant theater parties on Broadway, luncheons and bridge parties to benefit the Talmud Torah School. Substantial amounts were raised for United Jewish Appeal and the Red Cross. Jewish servicemen received Passover packages. Nowadays, theater parties and Sisterhood fundraising projects in general are much more modest in scale, both in terms of social outreach and actual funds raised. The Sisterhood also used to work with other organizations in civic efforts, such as an expansion drive to celebrate the Metropolitan Museum of Art Diamond Jubilee; and it participated in the work of an association to assist new Americans.

Victims of persecution were not forgotten -- those from Nazi Germany as well as those from Egypt and other Arab countries in the late 1950s and, more recently, since the 1970s, those from the Soviet Union..

Today, it is truly amazing to realize how so few are accomplishing so much with such scarce resources:

- The Sisterhood continues to be in charge of the Succah and the beautification of the Sanctuary during Shabuot.
- It supports the Joint Passover Association, the Passover Fund of the New York Board of Rabbis, Hatzoloh, Dorot and Keren Or.
- Bible classes have been a favorite for years.
- The Elsie Adlman Camp Fund enables many children to go to camp.
- Toys made by Sisterhood members are sent to local hospitals.
- Sisterhood supports Nahlah Dalton in Israel, named for Dr. David and Mrs. Tamar de Sola Pool. The Sisterhood liaison with Dalton, a longtime resident of Israel,

recently wrote that a winery has been established to make kiddush wine of excellent quality. It is sold in Israel and will be exported soon. A furniture factory is doing well and has just opened a new building. Some ground in the area is still available for further projects, and additional investors are being sought. The Sisterhood also provides scholarships for school children and one of its members, Rosa Pressel, has been most generous in providing funds for books and other things for the children.

The question is: Given the present circumstances, how long can this inspiring contribution continue?

The time has come to readapt. The challenge is to recognize a crisis which has been looming for more than a decade, to face the inevitability of change and to channel that change toward a new dynamic without losing our essential reason for being. In Giuseppe di Lampedusa's words, we need to change in order to remain the same.

THE RELIGIOUS VISION OF REVEREND DR. HENRY PEREIRA MENDES

by Marc D. Angel

D r. Mendes served as Minister of Congregation Shearith Israel from 1877 through 1920. He continued to be associated with the Congregation as Minister Emeritus until his death in 1937. During the course of these 60 years with Shearith Israel, Dr. Mendes established himself as a remarkable communal leader, scholar and author.

Born in Birmingham, England, Henry Pereira Mendes grew up in a family well-known for its history of producing religious leaders. Indeed, his father Abraham was Minister of the Jewish congregation in Birmingham. H.P. Mendes received his early religious education and inspiration from his parents and as a young man served as Hazan and Minister of the Sephardic congregation in Manchester. While in New York, he studied and graduated from the medical school of New York University. In 1890, he was married to Rosalie Rebecca Piza.

Dr. Mendes was proud to be the religious leader of the oldest Jewish congregation in North America. From this base, he promoted numerous communal and social ideals and causes.

He was one of the leading Orthodox rabbis in the United

States. Although he was Sephardic, he won the good will of the entire Orthodox community, including the Yiddish-speaking immigrants. He was a founder and the first president of the Union of Orthodox Jewish Congregations of America (1898). He also had been one of the founders of the Jewish Theological Seminary (1887), which he and his collaborators intended to be an institution which would produce English-speaking Orthodox rabbis.

While staunchly Orthodox, he worked with all Jews for the betterment of the community. He was among the founders of the New York Board of Rabbis and was one of the early presidents of the organization. In 1885, he helped organize a branch of the Alliance Israélite Universelle in New York. He also was instrumental in the founding of the YWHA in New York, as well as Montefiore Hospital and the Lexington School for the Deaf.

Dr. Mendes was proud of the fact that Theodore Herzl asked his cooperation in organizing the Zionist movement in the United States. Dr. Mendes was elected vice-president of the Federation of American Zionists and a member of the actions committee of the World Zionist Organization. He advocated "Bible Zionism" or "spiritual Zionism" - an idea of establishing a Jewish state founded upon the principles and ideals of the Jewish religious tradition.

A prolific author, Dr. Mendes wrote essays and editorials, children's stories, textbooks, sermons, prayers, dramatic works, poetry and commentaries. His writings were imbued with the love of the Bible.

Rabbi Bernard Drachman, a colleague of Dr. Mendes, described him as "an ideal representative of Orthodox Judaism." He praised Mendes' "absolute freedom...from anything approaching narrowness or sectarian bias within the Jewish community."

Dr. Mendes served Shearith Israel with outstanding devotion. He was a champion of the synagogue's traditions. At a time when reform and change were the popular catchwords, Dr. Mendes was an eloquent voice for tradition.

The religious vision of Dr. Mendes is reflected in the titles of his main books: *Jewish History Ethically Presented* (1895), *The Jewish Religion Ethically Presented* (1895), and *Jewish Life Ethically Presented* (1917). In 1934 he prepared a little volume of prayers and meditations for home use "to promote and facilitate the habit of prayer."

Dr. Mendes' religious outlook was deeply steeped in the Hebrew Bible. The verses of Scripture served as the basis of an ethical and compassionate way of life. *In The Jewish Religion Ethically Presented,* Dr. Mendes demonstrated his method of thought. He began each section with a citation from the Bible, and then provided the traditional lessons which were derived from the text. He then added his own elaboration of moral lessons which could be rooted in the biblical text. And then he offered a series of biblical quotations to close each section.

For example, in dealing with the third of the Ten Commandments (Thou shalt not take the name of the Lord thy God in vain; for the Lord will not hold him guiltless that taketh His name in vain), Dr. Mendes provided the traditional explanations of this commandment. It is forbidden to use God's name in a disrespectful way, for false oath or for any wrong purpose. Likewise, this commandment is violated whenever one says prayers without concentration and reverent devotion. Dr. Mendes added the ethical component:

"We take His name in vain, or to no purpose, if we speak of God being good, just, merciful, etc., without trying ourselves to be good, just, merciful, etc." We must be loving, merciful and forgiving, in emulation of God's ways.

Dr. Mendes then offered a number of extensions to this commandment: "We are children of God. We are called by His name. When we do wrong, we disgrace or profane His name. Hence a disgraceful act is called Chilul Hashem, a profanation of the Name. And just as all the members of a family feel any disgrace that any one of them incurs, so when any Hebrew does wrong, the disgrace is felt by all Jews. We are known as the people of God. We assume His name in vain unless we obey His Laws. ...We take or assume His name in vain when we call ourselves by His name and say we are His children or His people, while for our convenience or ease we neglect religious duties which He has commanded us" (*The Jewish Religion Ethically Presented*, revised edition, 1912, pp. 59-60).

In elaborating on the commandment to honor one's parents, Dr. Mendes stated: "To honor parents, ministers of religion, the aged, the learned, our teachers and authorities is a sign of the highest type of true manliness and of true womanliness. Respect for parents is essential to the welfare of society. ...Anarchy or the absence of respect for authority, always brings ruin. Respect for all the authorities is insisted upon in the Bible" (p. 64).

In discussing the commandment prohibiting murder, Dr. Mendes noted that "we may not kill a man's good name or reputation, nor attack his honor. We do so when we act as tale-bearer or slanderer." He goes on to say that "we may not kill a man's business. ...Respect for human life carries with it respect for anyone's livelihood. We may not make it hard for others to live by reason of our own greed" (pp. 65-66).

Dr. Mendes constantly emphasized the need for religion to be a steady and constant force in one's life. True religion is expressed not merely in ceremonials, but in our conduct in all aspects of our daily life. In his *Jewish Daily Life Ethically Presented* (1917), Dr. Mendes taught that "our religion thus requires threefold work from us: we must work for our own happiness, we must work for the happiness of the world we live in, and we must work for the glory of God. Our dietary laws mean healthy bodies and healthy minds to be able to do this threefold work" (p. 57). He argued that the laws of Kashruth are based on physical and ethical reasons and are designed to promote and conserve our physical health. The laws of Kashruth, by governing everything we eat, add a spiritual and ethical dimension to this basic human need.

Dr. Mendes wrote: "Our daily work, no matter how important or how menial, if we perform it conscientiously, becomes equivalent to an act of worship. It therefore means setting God before us as the One we desire to please by the faithful discharge of our daily duties. This kind of recognition of good faith, honesty and honor means religion. Conscientiousness is religion. We must therefore do our work conscientiously. We should derive spiritual happiness out of labor by recognizing that God consecrates labor (p. 59).

Dr. Mendes often expressed his philosophy in witty epigrams. A number of these were collected by Dr. David de Sola Pool in his biography of Dr. Mendes. The following are some examples of Dr. Mendes' wit and wisdom:

In too many homes religion is a farce, not a force.

I plead, let every man and woman privately commune with God to place his or her heart-needs before Him.

I plead for Sabbath observance.

The three greatest R's: Reverence, Righteousness and Responsibility.

Democracy is the ideal form of government, but it needs ideal citizens.

Music helps us find God.

Let us have less fault-finding, and more fault-mending.

Speak to the young; but first to the old.

To be accorded all of little Palestine is not too great a reward for having given the world the Bible.

Peace for the world at last and the realization of reverence for God by all men. These are the essentials for human happiness. Zionism stands for them.

Dr. Mendes was an avid Zionist; the focus of his Zionism was the religious and spiritual revival of the Jewish people, so that a Jewish state would become a spiritual inspiration to the entire world. He felt that the goals of Zionism could not be accomplished unless the Jews themselves were faithful to their religious traditions. Moreover, he believed it was necessary to win the support and respect of the non-Jewish world. "That respect we can have only if we respect ourselves by respecting our religion. Here is true work for Zionists: to keep Hebrews true to Jewish life, Jewish law, Jewish sentiment" (letter of Dr. Mendes to Haham Gaster, July 21, 1903, published in *Tradition*, Fall, 1995, p. 70).

In spite of his tireless efforts and his eloquent expositions, Dr. Mendes realized that many Jews were turning away from the Jewish religious traditions. Compromises in religious observance were being made for reasons of convenience or ideology. The level of serious Jewish learning was declining. He struggled with singular devotion to raise the Jewish people to a higher level of knowledge and observance, a deep-felt spirituality, a God-inspired ethical worldview.

In 1911, he delivered a sermon at Shearith Israel, after he had recovered from a serious illness. He reminisced about past challenges which he and the Congregation had faced together. "In looking over the years that have sped, there are times when I think that I have failed to bring religion's holy teachings into the hearts of all this Congregation, and therefore I have failed to do His will. ...I do know that I have failed to bring into the lives of all the members of the Congregation that spirituality which alone can make us all sons and daughters of God in the highest sense, that spirituality of life which makes us willing, eager, anxious to do His will....It is true, and I thank God for it, that many of you are working hard to bring religion into actual life. You strive to have your children as loyal as you are, and as your parents before you were; you strive to bring sunshine into the lives of others; your communal and congregational activities are splendid. ...But I repeat, I confess to failure in influencing the lives of those of this Congregation who rarely or never set foot in this holy building; who hold aloof from congregational and communal work; in whose homes Sabbath is forgotten, from whose homes all Jewish characteristics are banished; who forget that constant absence from Sabbath worship, gradually, insidiously, but invariably disintegrates the Jewishness of the home and of all its inmates, and invariably precedes that desertion from our religion which we understand by the expression 'he or she has married out.' ...Let us both try to prove our gratitude to God by doing His will. Then, come sorrow, come trial, come defeat, come death itself, the God who alone knows the human heart, who alone can read the inmost soul, shall judge whether you and I have labored in vain, whether you and I have spent our strength for naught, and in vain, - for surely our judgement shall be with the Lord and our work shall be before our God."

In his sixty years of association with Shearith Israel, Dr. Mendes faced many challenges and had many accomplishments. He was proud, yet modest; forceful, yet gentle; spiritual, yet practical. His memory has continued to influence and inspire the generations which have followed.

BIBLIOGRAPHY

Angel, Marc, "Mendes, Henry Pereira," in *Jewish-American History and Culture: An Encyclopedia*, edited by J. Fischel and S. Pinsker, New York and London, 1992, pp. 386-87.

Markovitz, Eugene, "Henry Pereira Mendes: Architect of the Union of Orthodox Jewish Congregations of America," *American Jewish Historical Quarterly*, Vol. 55 (1965), pp. 364-384. Markovitz, Eugene, "H. P. Mendes: Builder of Traditional Judaism in America," doctoral dissertation, Yeshiva University, 1961.

Pool, David and Tamar, *An Old Faith in the New World*, New York, 1955, pp. 192-201.

Pool, David de Sola, *H. Pereira Mendes: A Biography*, New York, 1938.

A VENERABLE CONGREGATION IN A NEW BUILDING: A LOOK INTO THE LIFE OF SHEARITH ISRAEL IN 1897

by: Jeffrey Gurock

INTRODUCTION

As a historian, it is a pleasure to address a congregation that possesses a strong sense of its own history, that has dedicated itself to preserving its historical record, and which has been led by scholar-rabbis like Henry Pereira Mendes - about whom I will have much to say presently - David de Sola Pool, and your present Rabbi Marc Angel, who have all been engaged, each in his own way and style, in the historical enterprise. Indeed, I shall rely on the work of your congregational chroniclers as complemented by my own understanding of the New York Jewish scene of one-hundred years ago, in identifying and discussing the challenges the then 225 year old congregation faced and the role it played in the evolution of Judaism and Orthodoxy in the metropolis.

In 1897, Shearith Israel was remarkable as a role model congregation that stressed both fidelity to the Halakhah and comfort with modernity. As we will soon see, Shearith Israel showed the way in maintaining its allegiance to its hallowed traditional ritual and in avoiding the fate of so many once-Orthodox congregations of its, and subsequent, times when it moved from the inner city towards suburbia. In 1897, Shearith Israel, stood out, through Rabbi Mendes' efforts, in the essential role it played in the founding of the Union of Orthodox Jewish Congregations of America (The Orthodox Union) which worked arduously to perpetuate Judaism among the masses downtown. Thus, 1897 proved to be a turning point year both in the internal and external life of this path-setting congregation.

AVOIDING CONGREGATIONAL FACTIONALISM IN "MEDURBIA"

The movement of Jews from the inner regions of cities towards the outer reaches of American metropolises - the part of town called "medurbia" in the parlance of one sociologist - has often not favored the maintenance of Orthodox traditions. The reality has been that so long as Jews were resident downtown and ensconced there in their ethnic cocoons, whatever their personal deviations from religious commitments, the power of the tradition coupled with a certain degree of unacculturation, usually combined to keep the fundamentals of Orthodox synagogue life intact. Rarely were calls heard downtown for men and women to sit together, nor for abridgement of the services, nor for altering the traditional Jewish calendar and clock to suit American ways of life. The great fissure, the noticeable and disputatious breaks with tradition within the synagogue, awaited moves to "medurbia." In these new neighborhoods, Jews aspired to be like and be accepted by their Gentile neighbors. One of their great fears was that non-Jewish friends would happen upon their synagogues and be put off by their foreign looking ritual. The pressure to conform to American styles of worship -

particularly the perceived need to mix the sexes during prayer - was often irresistible. Thus, when synagogue boards decided what their synagogues should look like in their new communities, they more often than not determined to build their commodious sanctuaries without *mehitzot*, in violation of traditional strictures.

To be sure, American Orthodoxy has not been without a response to these calls for change. While sure to oppose halakhic deviations in synagogue life, it has frequently adopted a highly accommodationist and sociologically - sophisticated approach towards convincing Jews in medurban and suburban communities that the future of the faith in America still lay with the Orthodox synagogue. The American Orthodox rabbinate and lay leadership emphasized *inclusion* when it said to Jews who were drifting away from the synagogue that whatever their personal commitment to observance of mitzvot, Orthodoxy was accepting of them and wanted them within its midst. These forward-thinking leaders also stood four square in support of *simulation* as they endeavored to admit the sociology and culture of America into synagogue life without doing violence to the Halakhah. Their message was that an Orthodox synagogue could stand for style and beauty and possess a palpable panache even as it upheld the substance of Jewish tradition. Simply put, no one would be ashamed to show what went on in the modern Orthodox synagogue, if and when Gentile friends happened by. Finally, Orthodoxy in "medurbia" and beyond, spoke tellingly about its commitment to *cooperation* with all Jews on wider communal issues that transcended theological disagreements. When the concerns were global and threats were real and present, the Orthodox view was that all Jews are one.

How do these medurban and suburban scenarios - that became so common and apparent during the early second half of the twentieth century - relate to the story of Shearith Israel in 1897? As with so many other events and issues in American Jewish history, this oldest congregation in the United States was a precedent setter. As we will now see, Shearith Israel moved out of the inner city of downtown Manhattan in the last years of the nineteenth century, faced up to the desire of some members to change, and held fast to its Orthodoxy.

In 1860, when Shearith Israel relocated from its third home on Crosby Street to 19th Street and Fifth Avenue, it was then centered in a prime residential district of private homes on the very outskirts of the downtown community. At that point, before the Civil War, Manhattan's reach as an urban metropolis extended only as far north as 42nd Street. The city's poorer elements lived south of Fourteenth Street. Immigrant Central Europeans and Central European Jews were situated east of the Bowery in what was emerging as the Lower East Side. Irish newcomers were ensconced primarily west of the Bowery in their own poor enclave. At this point, the uptown communities of the future, like Yorksville or Harlem or the West Side or Morningside Heights or Washington Heights, were basically farm land separated from the "city" by the absence of modern rapid transit links.

Over the succeeding thirty years, New York experienced fundamental and profound ecological and demographic changes. The expansion of the downtown immigrant communities under the impact of massive Southern and East European migration brought the ghetto all too close to 19th Street. Certainly those members who lived south of the synagogue increasingly had good reasons to seek accommodations elsewhere in the city if their own resources permitted migration. At the same time, the expansion of the city's rapid transit system, through the building of elevated railroads up the eastern and western spines of Manhattan facilitated those with the economic wherewithal and social confidence to move from downtown to new Manhattan communities. By the mid 1880's, a new uptown, north of 59th Street, was born composed of working class elements who settled in newly-constructed tenements both east of Park Avenue and west of Columbus Avenue complemented by communities of middle class brownstone dwellers who resided along Central Park West and within Park and Madison Avenues. Of course, there also was room uptown for mansions for the very wealthy that spanned Fifth Avenue as well as West End Avenue and Riverside. In all events, a substantial medurbia was created which inevitably attracted members of the Shearith Israel community to its midst.

By the 1890's, Shearith Israel was no longer a neighborhood synagogue, and congregational leaders were well aware of the problems and challenges that threatened their future. Indeed, as early as the 1880's, congregational leaders already were engaged in robust discussions about where, when and how to move the synagogue closer to where congregants increasingly were now resident. There was some talk of stationing the synagogue on 59th Street and Fifth Avenue (near today's Plaza Hotel). There was also a suggestion that Shearith Israel seek out Harlem, another incipient Jewish community of time. But, in the end, a sage decision was made to build a new beautiful and commodious building on 70th Street and Central Park West.

More importantly for us, as the congregation deliberated

over where the synagogue might be situated, a concomitant debate ensued over what type of synagogue they should have. Predictably, the pressure to reform the service - to make it more attractive, more respectable etc. - was real and present. After all, during this era, comparable congregational debates had taken place in any number of formerly Orthodox downtown synagogues that were destined to become landmark Reform Temples in the new uptown neighborhoods. Keeping up with the momentum towards Reform, advocates of change spoke of the need for mixed seating, of the importance of utilizing instrumental music to make the service more elegant, and there was talk too of shortening the service, all to project a more modern image.

Nonetheless, Shearith Israel, under the skilled guidance and influence of Rabbi Mendes, held the line against these anti-Orthodox efforts. And when congregational officials were polled about the necessity of maintaining separate seating in the new sanctuary - among the other basic requirements that distinguish the Orthodox synagogue - those in control reasserted by a ten to one margin that the old ways be maintained. It may well be that a petition submitted by 96 women of the congregation played a highly influential role in swaying leadership sentiment. In their brief, these women staunchly opposed the arguments harbored by advocates of change. The women asserted that seating the sexes together during praying would neither contribute to increased attendance by those drifting from synagogue life nor would it garner a greater "respect for the Hebrews in the eyes of the community." In the end, Orthodoxy won at Shearith Israel because traditionalists spoke proudly of the congregation's commitment to inclusion and simulation. Mendes and his followers were able to say that their accommodating and accepting synagogue was as decorous, as modern, and as contemporary looking as any Reform Temple. Moreover, they reassured everyone that through its style and substance, they would earn for the Jews of Central Park West the approbation of their neighbors.

For the record, one other essential political factor helped determine the outcome of this crucial synagogue decision. Prior to the moments of truth of 1897, the congregation put in place a committee that investigated the religious leanings of potential members to weed out possible insurgents who might not possess Shearith Israel's renowned sense of history nor its sentiments towards maintaining its time-honored rituals. Subsequently, a rule was passed that members had to be affiliated at least three years before they could be electors; and only electors could enact ritual changes.

ADDRESSING THE RELIGIOUS NEEDS OF DOWNTOWN JEWRY

But, holding the line of Orthodoxy, as Shearith Israel's members learned to live comfortably with their traditions in medurbia, was only half of that synagogue's story in 1897. As a widely-respected national Jewish leader, Rabbi Mendes committed himself and his congregation to what we would today call "out-reach" to other Jews and communities. Indeed, just a few months after moving to 70th Street, Shearith Israel's rabbi joined a small coterie of rabbis and lay people in inaugurating the Orthodox Union. Although the original mandate of the organization spoke explicitly of the need to fight against the declarations of Reform rabbis not in keeping with the teachings of the Torah, in reality, the prime focus of early Union activities centered around the religious dilemmas of disaffected ghetto youth in a community where Reform Judaism was largely unknown. In other words, at the crucial point in time, Mendes and others understood that disaffection was far more pervasive a problem for their community than any renegade conceptions of Judaism articulated by Reform leaders uptown.

Simply put, the problem was that for the masses of young Jews who were fired with the desire to advance and to be accepted in America, the Judaism of their parents was a troubling burden. In an American six day work week, where the Christian Sabbath was implicitly hallowed by Blue Laws, observance of the Jewish Sabbath was a particular hardship. In a country that demanded immigrant acculturation, public school education was a given. And there in these Temples of Americanization, in addition to teaching children the rudimentary three "rs", youngsters were inculcated with an ever deepening disrespect for their parents' culture and past. And after school was over, not only did the streets beckon with their own informal American culture, but so did the Christian settlements and missions that aspired to draw youngsters away from Judaism. To be sure, there existed a pervasive folk Orthodoxy downtown that could be found in the landsmanshaft synagogue. These shuls or shtibls meant much to the unacculturated Jews as they reminded them of the best of the old side. But such historical memories had no currency for the young people of the American generation.

At this juncture, Orthodox leadership was of two different minds on how to address these vexing problems. For most of the rabbis who had come here from Eastern Europe, the answer was staunch resistance to American culture and excoriation of those who did not adhere faithfully to the old ways. Unfortunately for them, as much as they demanded adherence to traditions and rejection of the ways of America, they could not control their community. And then there was the policy of the Orthodox Union with Rabbi Mendes at the lead. They said to the non-observant second generation Jew who felt compelled to violate the Sabbath what while we cannot approve of your personal deviance, we do want you to be with us and to partake of our modern, American Orthodox services when your schedule permits. Such was the philosophy and policy of the Jewish Endeavor Society, the youth wing of the Orthodox Union that Mendes encouraged to conduct Orthodox Sabbath afternoon services for young people after their work week ended.

Simultaneous to these inclusionary synagogue efforts, the Orthodox Union attempted to offset the pernicious influences of the public schools, the streets and the Christian settlements. Their answer was the modern talmud torah system that simulated, pedagogically, the good that Americanizing institutions had to offer. And while he was at it, Mendes took particular delight in working, with the assistance of Shearith Israel lay leader Albert Lucas, towards exposing the so-called "masked institutions"—the Christian missions that surreptitiously attempted to proselytize Jewish youngsters.

Significantly, in mounting their efforts, Orthodox Union leaders recruited as foot soldiers in their campaigns young men and women from downtown who were then students at the Jewish Theological Seminary. Indeed, individuals like Mordecai M. Kaplan, Herman Abramowitz, Elias L. Solomon and others, who later in their careers would be identified as advocates of Conservative and Reconstructionist Judaism, received very important in-service training as American rabbis within the Union's wide Orthodox tent. Such was just part of the spirit of cooperation that infused Mendes' turn of the century communal efforts.

Not incidentally, what the Orthodox Union did with, and on behalf of Seminary students had no small resonance among the students of the Rabbi Isaac Elchanan Theological Seminary, the other all-important American Orthodox institution that came into existence at that same time. Young men at that yeshiva saw how Seminary men were learning how to relate to Americanized Jewish audiences and they wanted such training for themselves as well. They felt that since they possessed Torah training superior to Seminary men they could relate better to the older generation. And if they could receive the in-service training they desired, they could bridge the gap between generations. Ultimately, the yeshiva's leaders saw the wisdom of these demands. One sign that the Orthodox Union's idea did, in fact, sink into the yeshiva community, was first observable in 1915, when RIETS' first permanent president Dr. Bernard Revel appointed Dr. Henry P. Mendes as his school's first professor of homiletics.

All told, 1897 was a year where Shearith Israel reasserted itself as a role model Orthodox congregation and helped set patterns of inclusion, simulation and cooperation that held American Orthodoxy in good stead for the next half century and more. These are also traditions that this venerable congregation and its present scholar-rabbi live by today as Shearith Israel prepares to enter the 21st Century and approaches its 350th anniversary of service to the American Jewish Community.

AN APPRECIATION OF JUSTICE

BENJAMIN NATHAN CARDOZO*

by Judith S. Kaye

For more than a quarter century, Shearith Israel has been a spiritual home for Stephen and me, for our children and now for our grandchildren. As we all grow older together, we have shared with our friends here so many life milestones, including times of deepest sorrow and times of greatest joy. Today, *Shabbat Behar* in the year 5755, you have our special thanks for a day that always will be a memorable one for Stephen and me, for our son Jonathan (who read the *Haftarah*), and for all the Kayes. We are grateful beyond words for the singular honor you have allowed us.

Those of you who carry the Sephardic pocket diary close to your hearts, as Stephen and I do, know that *Shabbat Behar* is also an unusually important day in the life of this Congregation. On this day, in 1897-98 years ago-the building in which we are now gathered was consecrated....

It is incredible to think how events since 1897-including several wars, the creation of the State of Israel, and social and

* I am most grateful to my Law Clerk Roberta A. Kaplan for her superb support and assistance in the preparation of these remarks.

technological revolutions-have transformed the world outside these walls while the world within them remains essentially unchanged. This building has indeed been a sanctuary in both senses of the word - both a place of worship *and* a refuge from injustice and tragedy. For that reason alone, it is fitting on this day to pay respects to our predecessors who secured this cherished place for us and for generations to come.

There is yet another reason why this is a particularly memorable time-another event in this Congregation's unique history-and that is the 125th anniversary of the birth of one of our predecessors, Benjamin Nathan Cardozo, on May 24, 1870. Shearith Israel knows Cardozo as a lifelong member, as were his parents, and his many maternal and paternal ancestors dating back to the 1700's. His family includes several Presidents and Ministers of the Congregation such as his great granduncle, Reverend Gershom Mendes Seixas, who in August 1776 fled New York City with the Holy Scrolls to escape the invading British forces,[1] and it continues with children and grandchildren of cousins who are among us today. We know Cardozo as a bar mitzvah, an elector, a cousin, a friend. Surely he was present in this sanctuary, as a young attorney contemplating his 27th birthday, on that historic spring day in 1897 when the perpetual lamp was first lit and the scrolls of the Holy Law first placed in the Ark.

To members of this Congregation, Benjamin Cardozo may be remembered as dear friend and devoted family member, even a sort of pen pal to some, writing long letters in a distinctive cursive script that is on exhibit here today. But to the world, he is a monumental, towering figure-one of the greatest jurists of all time. To be called a "Cardozo," in legal circles, to be equated in any way with him, is the highest compliment a lawyer or judge could receive.

Perhaps even more important than his stunning powers of language and logic were his personal integrity and humility, his gentleness and sweetness, almost a saintliness that radiates even from pictures of him. Judge Learned Hand, when he was Chief Judge of the federal appellate court in New York, perhaps best described his friend Cardozo in these words: "He was wise because his spirit was uncontaminated, because he knew no violence, or hatred, or envy, or jealousy, or ill-will. I believe it was this purity that chiefly made him the judge we so much revere; more than his learning, his acuteness and his fabulous industry."[2] Similar thoughts were expressed about his cousin by our late *Parnas,* Judge Edgar J. Nathan, Jr., who wrote of this "sensitively modest man:" "Justice Cardozo aspired to no office, he sought not fame. But he labored with single-minded love and devotion in the profession he chose."[3]

Exemplifying Cardozo's humble and unassuming nature, Judge Hand reported that one day after lunch they both decided to look up something in the Public Library, but soon realized that the book they were looking for was extremely rare and thus kept under lock and key. Hand suggested that they go right to the director's office and arrange for an attendant to bring the book, as he usually did in such situations. Cardozo asked quietly, "Do you?" "Yes, to save time. Do you disapprove?" {Cardozo} smiled, "I wait in line," he said. "Your time is too valuable for the public," {Hand} countered. "I don't know about that," answered {Cardozo}. "As a citizen I take my turn."[4]

Cardozo was born into and unquestionably shaped by the values of this Congregation, his home imbued with the spirit of Judaism. Tutored by none other than Horatio Alger,

Cardozo graduated from Columbia College at the age of 19. After study at Columbia Law School, he entered his family's law firm, where he established a stellar reputation as a lawyer's lawyer. One friend said of his skills as a practicing attorney that: "He was unfitted for any struggle where scrupulous integrity and fine sense of what is right might be a handicap; but judges felt the persuasive force of his legal argument, and lawyers and laymen sought his counsel and assistance in the solution of intricate legal problems."[5]

Cardozo was elected a trial judge in 1913, but immediately elevated to New York's highest court-the Court of Appeals. For nearly three decades, he served as a Judge and then Chief Judge of the Court of Appeals - and after that, until his untimely death in 1938, as a Justice of the United States Supreme Court in Washington, all those years writing opinions and essays about the law and the judicial process that to this very day are exemplary.

As you may know, like Cardozo, I serve as the Chief Judge of the Court of Appeals, and even have the honor of occupying the desk that was his at the Courthouse in Albany. Having mentioned the title Chief Judge and the desk in Albany, I cannot help but note another Cardozo legacy, which resulted from his impassioned opposistion to the idea of mixed seating in this synagogue. The minutes of an electors' meeting in 1895-a century ago-reflect that Cardozo delivered "a long address, impressive in ability and eloquence" against a proposal to eliminate separate seating in the new building.[6]

What an irony it is that, thanks in part to the persuasive powers of a former Chief Judge, the current Chief Judge now sits upstairs.[7]

Before I go on about Judge Cardozo, allow me to turn to

the Torah reading which I followed earlier this morning from my seat upstairs. Today's portion is from the Book of Leviticus, which is in a sense a sort of manual, a guidebook of detailed instructions which enabled the Priests and Levites to perform the various rites that were required of them. The oldest name for the Third Book of Moses, in fact, is *"Torat Cohanim"* - "The Law of Priests."

Yet within this recitation of rules and procedures about subjects such as sacrifice and mitzvot, today's portion sounds a strikingly different note. It deals instead with matters of broader social, commercial, even environmental ethics - how we must treat our land, our relatives, our servants, our neighbors. The verses of *Behar,* when read against the technical passages that surround them, are unique in their deep concern about, for lack of a better term, the "underdog" - the slave, the indigent, the stranger.

Indeed, words taken from *Behar* - "You shall proclaim liberty throughout the land for all its inhabitants"[8] appear on this nation's Liberty Bell in Philadelphia. In fact, in the patriotic sermon he delivered in support of the American Revolution just prior to leaving New York City in 1776, Reverend Seixas spoke of the newly-cast Liberty Bell, urging that this Congregation not be "untrue to the tenets of George Washington, or sound a discordant note in opposition to the challenging and inspiring music of the Liberty Bell."[9] It is thus yet another distinction of this Shabbat for Shearith Israel that these words of *Behar* are inscribed on the special *rimonim,* replicas of the Liberty Bell, that we used during today's service.

It is, of course, not possible to speak of liberty without also speaking about justice. How many times have we recited the

Pledge of Allegiance, concluding "with liberty and justice for all." A central lesson of *Pessah,* celebrated just a few weeks ago, is that there is no justice without liberty. And indeed Benjamin Nathan Cardozo, who bore the title Justice, through his words and deeds, has become the very embodiment of the term.[10]

My own review of Cardozo's work leads me to conclude that in his heart he truly believed that law and justice are, or should be, synonymous, that-in his own words-"[t]he final cause of law is the welfare of society. The rule that misses its aim cannot permanently justify its existence."[11] Justice, according to Cardozo, "is so much of morality as the thought and practice of a given epoch shall conceive to be appropriately invested with a legal sanction...."[12] Cardozo believed that as the law evolves, "[t]he moral norm and the jural [are] brought together and are one."[13]

Though widely known as a Sephardic Jew, Cardozo, at a commencement address delivered at the Jewish Institute of Religion on his 61st birthday, acknowledged that he was unable to claim that the beliefs of the students there assembled were "wholly [his]" or "that the devastating years have not obliterated youthful faiths."[14] In a letter to a friend two years before his death, Cardozo noted: "I think a good deal these days about religion, wondering what it is and whether I have any. As the human relationships which make life what it is for us begin to break up, we search more and more for others that transcend them."[15]

Despite this admission, Cardozo did not at any time in his life shrink from holding "fast to certain values transcending the physical and temporal."[16] So, in our own body of law, he wrote, "the standard to which we appeal is sometimes characterized as that of justice, but also as the equitable, the fair, the thing consistent with good conscience,"[17] "the principle and practice of men and women of the community whom the social mind would rank as intelligent and virtuous."[18] Although I doubt that Cardozo had it in mind, I am struck by the similarity between his formulation of justice and the Torah's commandment that [Y]ou shall do what is right and good ... good-in the eyes of the Lord; right-proper in the eyes of men."[19]

In fact, for Cardozo, the very act of choice, of choosing "between competing and conflicting values,"[20] choosing the path of righteousness, was the highest form of human achievement. As he wrote "[t]he heroic hours of life do not announce their presence by drum and trumpet, challenging us to be true to ourselves....Some little, unassuming, unobtrusive choice presents itself before us slyly and craftily, glib and insinuating, in the modest garb of innocence. To yield to blandishments is so easy. The wrong, it seems, is venial. Only hyper-sensitiveness, we assure ourselves, would call it wrong at all. These are moments when you will need to remember the game that you are playing. Then it is that you will be summoned to show the courage of adventurous youth...."[21]

I have no doubt that Cardozo himself was well acquainted with those "little, unassuming, unobtrusive moments," those times when an easy choice could be made, a choice to do something that at first doesn't seem all that wrong and will likely go unnoticed, something that might even be more popular than the more difficult but truly correct and honorable decision. Cardozo certainly faced such dilemmas every day he donned his judicial robes, and given his vast intellectual powers, there is no question that he could readily have yielded to the easier path. But the true test of a judge for him was the extent to which he fulfilled "the correspondence between law and justice....not in fair weather, but in foul, in times of stress and strain, when the legal mechanism should hold good against passion and prejudice and cruelty, and show what it can do."[22] It is precisely because he held out "in times of stress and strain," because he struggled to make exactly the right decision when faced with difficult questions of right and wrong, that Cardozo is to this day acclaimed as one of our greatest jurists.

In a radio broadcast delivered over station WHN just weeks after Cardozo's death, Hand described Cardozo's decisionmaking process in Biblical terms: "At times to those of us who knew him, the anguish which had preceded decision was apparent, for again and again, like Jacob, he had to wrestle with the angel all through the night; and he wrote his opinion with his very blood."[23] One of Cardozo's biographers provided a similar description when he stated that: "[t]he opinions of Cardozo on the bench in New York and on the Supreme Court at Washington show his aversion from any judgement essentially unethical, humanly unfair. At the same time, his respect for the law as a whole never abated, and so he was wrestling with problems involved in this duel between legalism and the higher justice."[24]

In studying the verses of *Behar* in preparation for today, I was struck by how much of the Torah's precepts even in those few verses from Leviticus, can be seen in Cardozo's work. Cardozo himself unwittingly commented upon this phenomenon in a college essay about the poet Matthew Arnold when he wrote: "[t]he works of any man must always partake, in large degree, of the spirit of the man himself; and the more pronounced and earnest his views may be, the more the truths he has discerned burden him and press for utterance, the more constantly will they dominate his writings, and the more clearly will his writings reflect the workings of his spirit."[25]

A passage from today's Torah portion, for example, commands that "[w]hen you sell property to your neighbor, or buy any from your neighbor, you shall not wrong one another....Do not wrong one another, but fear your God; for I the Lord am your God."[26] I think Cardozo had similar thoughts when he wrote in a case involving a dispute between business partners that "[m]any forms of conduct permissible in a workaday world for those acting at arm's length, are forbidden to those bound by fiduciary ties. A trustee is held to something stricter than the morals of the market place. Not honesty alone, but the punctilio of an honor the most sensitive, is then the standard of behavior."[27]

In a well-known contract dispute, Cardozo wrote that "there will be no assumption of a purpose to visit venial faults with oppressive retribution."[29]

Another passage from today's portion concerns the treatment of strangers and the poor: "If your kinsman, being in straits, comes under your authority, and you hold him as though a resident alien, let him live by your side: do not exact from him advance or accrued interest, but fear your God. Let him live by your side as your kinsman. Do not lend him money at advance interest, or give him your food at accrued interest."[30]

Again, I sense that similar values inspired Cardozo's thinking in a case allowing an Austrian citizen living in the United States to recover under her father's will despite the anti-German hysteria at the beginning of the First World War. In Cardozo's words, "I find nothing incompatible with the policy of the government, with the safety of the nation....so as to sustain plaintiff's title. We do not confiscate the lands or goods of the stranger within our gates."[31]

Perhaps the most poignant example of Cardozo's wisdom and compassion was a case refusing to remove the custody of a two year old girl from her improverished immigrant parents and award it instead to a rich couple with whom she had been living while her aunt worked as their housekeeper.[32] As Cardozo wrote-over the dissent of two of his colleagues: "Undoubtedly, the inference is permissible...that the father and mother were willing for the time being to leave the child with generous folk of ample means who were anxious to have her with them and to care for her as their own....[T]he [child's] parents...may have weakly hesitated. They may have foolishly delayed. They may have drifted into a situation where their desires and expectations were open to misconception....All that is not enough. They must have been found to have renounced. The petitioners would have us hold that what began, so to speak, as a loan, was thereafter transformed into a gift and this though a readiness to give had been explicitly disclaimed. We cannot say that silence and inaction were prolonged to such a point that an intention to surrender becomes an inference to law."[33]

It is hard to think of a better manifestation-in secular law-of *Behar's* injunction that "[if] your kinsman, being in straits, comes under your authority, and you hold him as though a resident alien, let him live by your side: do not exact from him advance or accrued interest, but fear your God." As Cardozo noted in another context, "the jural norm, however much it might disguise itself under a strict construction of the bond [does] not in truth ignore the quality of mercy."[34]

The verses of *Behar* contain instructions concerning the observance of two sanctified years, the Seventh Year or *Shemittah* when the land was to rest and lie fallow and the Fiftieth or Jubilee Year when all Hebrew slaves were to be emancipated and property returned to its original owners. One peculiar feature of the *Shemittah*, or the seventh year, was the requirement of a remission of debts, with the outstanding principal due on loans among the Israelites released and remitted to the debtor.[35]

As one might expect, however, because of this strict requirement, as the seventh year approached, potential creditors became increasingly reluctant to lend funds since the loans would soon have to be forgiven. Hillel, realizing that this unfortunate state of affairs was causing those in need to suffer, devised a solution whereby on the year of the *Shemittah*, the debt was assigned to the Court, which since it was not "a fellow" of the debtor could continue to hold the loan thus preserving the incentive to make loans to the needy. As the Talmud later explained this *halakhic* "innovation:" "The Rabbis have power to expropriate property should it be for the general public good."[36]

Like Hillel, Cardozo also recognized that innovation in the law is at times necessary so that the law may better serve the common good and he did not hesitate to say so.[37] In a time when the proper role of judges was perceived to be merely to apply existing legal rules, such candid expressions by a sitting judge were startling, even revolutionary.[38] Cardozo believed that in each case, a court "must consider the reason of the rule and the evils which it aims to remedy."[39] Or, as he explained in an essay he called "The Growth of the Law" - "Law must be stable, and yet it cannot stand still. Here is the great antinomy confronting us at every turn. Rest and motion, unrelieved and unchecked, are equally destructive."[40]

In preparing for today, I asked myself what lessons Cardozo's life, for all its brilliance and distinction in the law, has for us. Why speak of him here? One answer is that as a people we are of course defined by our history. As Jews and as members of this Congregation, it therefore is entirely fitting that we study our distinctive past and take pride in the outstanding contributions of one of our own. This great man, who through the Nathan and Cardozo families also brings together so much of the history of Shearith Israel and Jews in America, has surely earned a special place of honor in our thoughts and in our memory.

But there is more. It seems to me that the same "little, unassuming, unobtrusive" yet ultimately life-defining choices described by Cardozo-choices of right and wrong, of compassion and logic, choices that summon us, often "slyly and craftily," toward heroism or venality-present themselves to every one of us every day, whether we're sitting in a courtroom, in an office, or in our own homes. To prepare ourselves for those unannounced yet critical moments, so that we can recognize them and know in advance how to make the good and the right choices, is a reason both for studying Torah and for seeking justice through law.

But even that sentiment Cardozo expressed best. I'd like to conclude with his eloquent words addressed to those graduating rabbinical students: "You will find mockery and temptation on the highways, and for the values that you hold to be eternal many a tinsel token will be offered in exchange....Then will be the time when you will need to bethink yourselves of the values that were chosen by the prophets and saints of Israel, and by the goodly and noble of every race....When the course is finished, when the task is ended, when the books are closed, may the last appraisal of all values reveal [their] choices as yours.[41]

POSTSCRIPT

As an appellate judge, I am accustomed to distilling difficult thoughts into comprehensible prose: that at least is an objective of my responsibility as Chief Judge. That certain experiences can defy words was for me amply proven on Saturday, May 20, 1995, when, after the close of the service, I delivered my remarks in the sanctuary. As a woman and as a long-time member of Shearith Israel, I saw the deep emotion I felt reflected in the faces of my friends, burning into my mind the enormity of the privilege I was being allowed. I herewith return all expressions of appreciation I have received. Plainly, the thanks more appropriately go from me to each of you, most especially to Rabbi Marc Angel, who both proposed and persisted in the idea of my giving a talk.

NOTES

1. George S. Hellman, *Benjamin N. Cardozo: American Judge* 17-18 (1940).

2. Learned Hand, "Mr. Justice Cardozo," 52 Harv. L. Rev. 361,363 (1939).

3. Edgar J. Nathan, Jr., "Benjamin Nathan Cardozo," *The American Jewish Yearbook 5700*, p.28 (1939).

4. Hellman, *Cardozo* at 67-68.

5. Lehman, "A Memorial," reprinted in *Selected Writings of Benjamin Nathan Cardozo* xi (M. Hall ed. 1947) [hereinafter, *Selected Writings*].

6. Andrew L. Kaufman, "Benjamin N. Cardozo, Sephardic Jew." reprinted in *The Jewish Justices of the Supreme Court Revisited: Brandeis to Fortas* (Supreme Court Historical Society 1994).

7. The idea of a woman Chief Judge was surely unimaginable in the year 1895-25 years before women even had the right to vote and 88 years before the first woman was appointed to the Court. As a judge, Cardozo wisely foresaw a good deal about modern society, including the enormous potential of the automobile. *See e.g. MacPherson v. Buick,* 217 N.Y. 382 (1916). As a member of this Congregation, however, the principle of separate seating was for Cardozo one of religious and familial tradition.

8. Leviticus 25:10.

9. Hellman, *Cardozo* at 17-18.

10. In fact, a collection of Cardozo's writings published in the year of his death is aptly titled "Law *Is* Justice: Notable Opinions of Mr. Justice Cardozo." *See Law Is Justice: Notable Opinions of Mr. Justice Cardozo* (A.L. Sainer ed. 1938). As the editor of that book wrote: "To the student of the law, any decision by Mr. Justice Cardozo, has been proof that "law" is synonymous with "justice." *Id.* at *xi.*

11. Cardozo, "The Nature of the Judicial Process" reprinted in *Selected Writings* at 133.

12. Cardozo, "Paradoxes of Legal Science," reprinted in Selected Writings at 276.

13. *Id* at 277.

14. Cardozo, "Values: Commencement Address or The Choice of Tycho Brahe," reprinted in *Selected Writings* at 1.

15. Hellman, *Cardozo* at 264-65. Left for another day is a fuller response to those who would question Cardozo's lifelong devotion to Judaism, not as a matter of cultural identity-which none question-but rather as a matter of religious conviction. Briefly, as is evident from the tenor of this essay, I have little doubt that from his birth into our Congregation until the fulfillment of his last wish to be buried in acccordance with Sephardic ritual, Cardozo remained a committed Jew. I reach this conclusion based on his identification as a Jew by the outside world, his Jewish education, his home, his writings, his close ties to and constant communication with active members of the Congregation,

and his continued active membership in Jewish organizations. Though there surely were openly Orthodox Jews who achieved prominence in American legal and political circles in the pre-Holocaust world in which Cardozo lived, it would be wrong to view some of his expressions of inner struggle from the hindsight of today where the "melting pot" is no longer the dominant cultural metaphor, and wrong to forget that when appointed to the Supreme Court in 1932, a fellow Justice refused even to shake his hand. See Oscar Kraines, "Antisemitism on the Supreme Court Bench," *Mainstream* 12-15 (Jan. 1995).

16. Cardozo, "Values: Commencement Address," reprinted in *Selected Writings* at 1.

17. Cardozo, "The Paradoxes of Legal Science," reprinted in *Selected Writings* at 275.

18. *Id* at 274.

19. Arnold Cohen, *An Introduction to Jewish Civil Law* 145-46 (1991).

20. Cardozo, "Values: Commencement Address," reprinted in *Selected Writings* at 6.

21. Cardozo, "Law and Literature," reprinted in *Selected Writings* at 419.

22. Cardozo, "Our Lady of the Common Law" reprinted in *Selected Writings* at 92.

23. Learned Hand, "Mr. Justice Cardozo," 52 Harv. L. Rev. at 362.

24. Hellman, *Cardozo* at 47.

25. Cardozo, "The Moral Element in Matthew Arnold," reprinted in *Selected Writings* at 61.

26. Leviticus 25:14.

27. *Meinhard v. Salmon*, 249 N.Y. 458 (1928).

28. *Jacobs & Young v. Kent* 230 N.Y. 239, 242 (1921).

29. *Matter of Reisfeld*, 227 N.Y. 137, 140 (1919).

30. Leviticus 25: 35-37.

31. *Techt v. Hughes*, 229 N.Y. 222, 244 (1920).

32. *Matter of Bistany*, 239 N.Y. 19 (1924).

33. *Id* at 23.

34. Cardozo, "Paradoxes of Legal Science, reprinted in *Selected Writings* at 276.

35. Cohen, *An Introduction to Jewish Civil Law* at 72-76.

36. *Id* at 74.

37. Others have noted this affinity in outlook between Cardozo and Hillel. See Myriam J. Altman, "The Lessons of Justice Cardozo," *New York Law Journal,* Apr. 7, 1995, p.2. Cardozo, like Hillel, believed in the concept "that when a rule, after it has been duly tested by experience, has been found to be inconsistent with the sense of justice or with the social welfare, there should be less hesitation in its abandonment." Cardozo, "The Nature of the Judicial Process," reprinted in *Selected Writings* at 171. *See also* Grant Gilmore, *The Ages of American Law* 74-78 (1974); Norman Lamm & Aaron Kirschenbaum, "Freedom and Constraint in the Jewish Judicial Process," 1 Cardozo L. Rev. 99-133 (1979).

38. G. Gilmore, *Ages of American Law* at 77 ("The thing that is hardest to imagine about [Cardozo's] *The Nature of the Judicial Process* is the furor which its publication caused....Cardozo's hesitant confession that judges were, on rare occasions, more than simple automata, that they made law instead of merely declaring it, was widely regarded as a legal version of hardcore pornography.").

39. *Matter of Fowles,* 222 N.Y. 222, 233 (1918).

40. Cardozo, "The Growth of the Law," reprinted in *Selected Writings* at 186.

41. Cardozo, "Values: Commencement Address," reprinted in *Selected Writings* at 6.

ARCHITECTURE AND VISUAL ARTS

OF THE SPANISH AND PORTUGUESE SYNAGOGUE

OF NEW YORK CITY*

by Ronda Angel Arking

T he Spanish and Portuguese Synagogue of New York, Congregation Shearith Israel, was founded in 1654, the first Jewish congregation in North America. Its rituals derive from the practices of Jews from Spain and Portugal from before the expulsion of 1492. Yet the flavor of these rituals is distinctly American, as the ritual objects, as well as the architectural design of the building, reflect American aesthetic sensibility. The American nature of the visual arts of the Spanish and Portuguese Synagogue, together with the Sephardic meaning of the traditions, lend to a service which combines vastly different cultures through an aesthetic medium.

The Spanish and Portuguese Synagogue's history, as well as its architecture, music, and decorative arts, contribute to its position as an American cultural, aesthetic, and religious institution. In this article, I will provide a brief historical

* Reprinted from *Haham Gaon Memorial Volume*, ed. M.D. Angel, New York, 1997.

context of the arts of Shearith Israel and discuss the present building's visual and cultural characteristics.

LATE NINETEENTH CENTURY RELIGIOUS ARCHITECTURE

By the late 1880s, the Gothic and Romanesque revival had replaced the Classical as the most popular styles for synagogues. Moorish architecture had become very popular among the German Reform community and began to spread as a stylish form of synagogue architecture.[1]

Arnold William Brunner (1857-1925), the architect of the Seventieth Street building of the Spanish and Portuguese Synagogue (dedicated in 1897), was trained at MIT and was probably the first American-born Jewish architect. He also designed the State Department Building in Washington, the Cadet Hospital at West Point, and the School of Mines at Columbia University, among other buildings. In 1893, he attended an architectural exposition and conference where it was decided that classical architecture was acceptable for secular buildings, but the Romanesque and Gothic revival styles were more appropriate for religious buildings. But rather than adhere to the contemporary trends in religious architecure, Brunner looked to the past buildings of the Spanish and Portuguese Synagogue in order to create a building which would reflect the congregation's history, not the trends of modernity.

The classical architectural history of the Spanish and Portuguese Synagogue begins with its Mill Street Synagogue (built in 1730), with a Gregorian interior and neo-classical references. It continues with the Greek revival Crosby Street Synagogue of 1834 and the Nineteenth Street Synagogue of

1860[2] with the layering of Ionic and Corinthian orders. In his article, "Arnold Brunner's Spanish and Portuguese Synagogue: Issues of Reform and Reaffirmation in Late Nineteenth-Century America"[3] Maurice Berger argues that

> while the Mill, Crosby, and to some extent the Nineteenth Street buildings were designed in the neo-classical styles popular in their period of construction, the Seventieth Street building represents a total departure from contemporaneous synagogue design.

Brunner's concern for history and tradition surpassed the influences of contemporary trends in architecture. In Brunner's own writings regarding the design of the Seventieth Street building, he notes that

> the choice for ecclesiastical buildings now, broadly speaking, lies between two great styles - Gothic and Classic. I am unhesitatingly of the opinion that the latter is the one that is best fit and proper for the synagogue in America. With the sanction of antiquity it perpetuates the best traditions of Jewish art and takes up a thread, which was broken by circumstances, of a vigorous and once healthy style (Berger 166).

Shearith Israel resisted new forms of architectural expression for its own synagogue building. Judaism in the late nineteenth century was being pulled in two opposite directions - toward maintaining tradition and toward assimilation. Placing the Spanish and Portuguese Synagogue amidst this struggle, Berger asserts:

> As a testament to this crucial period, the Spanish and Portuguese Synagogue innately symbolized the great theological issue of nineteenth-century American Jewry - the polemic between the forces of reform and reaffirmation (164).

Berger goes on to argue that "the selection of a Moorish, Romanesque, or Gothic design, styles popular in the German

Reform community, would have suggested acknowledgment, if not outright acceptance, of the Reform influence" (166). In the late nineteenth century, architectural form defined a religious and political affiliation. This had the effect of either welcoming or alienating members of the community, and made concrete the identity of a given community.

Architecture suggests theology and philosophy. It is a form of expression which describes, to some extent, the people it contains. When discussing synagogue architecture from a religious perspective, we can look to the Bible for examples of how much time, energy, artistry, and material resources went into the building of the Tabernacle and Solomon's Temple. These examples of architecture as a representation of a culture, as an art form requiring much planning and artistic expertise, serve as a model to architects of religious buildings. A synagogue not only defines a particular community's philosophy; it also serves as a house of God. What a community considers fit for this purpose is reflective of its theology as well. The choice of architectural design for a nineteenth-century synagogue reflected political, religious, and historical considerations.

The classical style of Shearith Israel describes its ties to ancient traditions and inheritances, as well as its own history as an American synagogue. The services of the Spanish and Portuguese Synagogue are completely traditional; the prayers derive from biblical tradition, religious poetry, and rabbinic writings. In late nineteenth century America, the hold of tradition was weakening among many members of the Jewish community. Thus, the ancient focus of the architecture of the Spanish and Portuguese Synagogue stresses adherence to traditional Jewish culture and practice. Authority is found in antiquity; authority is found in ancient Jewish tradition; the synagogue is itself a reflection of authority rooted in history. The classical architecture of the Seventieth Street building also maintains the continuum of classical references within the synagogue's own history.

Also reflective of a Jewish community's philosophy is the interior design of its synagogue. According to Spanish and Portuguese custom, the benches in the synagogue run laterally along the sides of the building, perpendicular to the Ark of the Torahs. The *Tebah,* or reader's platform and desk, sits in the back-center of the sanctuary, facing the Ark with no object or piece of furniture coming between it and the Ark on the east wall. This serves an aesthetic purpose, emphasizing the clean sweep of the architecture. It also has religious meaning: the lack of interfering objects or benches is said to allow the hazzan's (cantor) or rabbi's voice of prayer to be directed toward the Torah Ark, the most sacred part of the sanctuary, with no intervening barriers.

> As David and Tamar de Sola Pool note in *An Old Faith in a New World,* the liturgy, the ritual, and the music of Congregation Shearith Israel have maintained unbroken the fundamental tradition of Western European Sephardim that was developed during a millennium of life in Spain successively under Visigothic, Moslem and Christian rule.[4]

The survival of these traditions is echoed in the classical architecture. Even the name of the congregation, Shearith Israel (Remnant of Israel), suggests its ancient roots as part of the original people of Israel. Many of the chants and prayers sung in the services date back to antiquity. However, the Spanish and Portuguese Synagogue is situated in a modern context and has always been involved with contemporary social, political, and educational issues. The ancient references of the synagogue's art and ritual suggest a place whence to begin to express religious feelings and social imperatives.[5]

ARCHITECTURE AND MEANING;
THE SEVENTIETH STREET SANCTUARY

When one enters the sanctuary of the Spanish and Portuguese Synagogue, one recognizes the large scale and grandness of this interior; yet one is not totally overwhelmed. In contrast, Gothic monumental architecture has the effect of erasing physical presence; it leads one's eyes and thoughts upward, toward high stained-glass panels, toward the point in the arch where both sides of the building merge. Standing in Shearith Israel's sanctuary, one cannot help but be aware of the physical in such a solid and geometrically balanced space.

Though the ornately carved coffered ceiling of the sanctuary is high, its rectangular shape and its symmetry make it knowable. The stained glass, crafted by the Louis Comfort Tiffany studios, like the ceiling, is visible and knowable. Unlike Gothic stained-glass panels, there is no narrative or message to decode in the windows, and rather than seeming to float in a lofty sphere, the windows extend from eye level in the men's section past the top row in the women's balcony. These monumental windows are symmetrical (though variations in the colors in the glass inevitably exist). The parts of the window closest to the ground have earthier tones than do the higher portions which contain more shades of blue and green. The difference in brightness of the upper and lower sections of the windows is probably a result of the exposure of the higher sections to more sunlight, but it is intriguing nonetheless that the division in color - earth tones/sky tones - creates the impression of a natural environment even in a highly crafted and manipulated environment.

These windows serve to contain the worshipper's vision within the walls of the sanctuary. The windows are not transparent, nor are they metaphors for a higher message or transcendent concept. Rather, their balanced geometry and muted colors create a boundary, focusing the eyes of the viewer toward the Ark, the Torah, and the prayer book - the main means for transcendence in this context.

The notions of knowledge, balance, and reason are predominant in the geometry and symmetry of the architecture. Unlike other late nineteenth century synagogues which incorporate symbols associated with Jewish culture, such as the Star of David, the Spanish and Portuguese Synagogue limits religious decoration to the Ten Commandments and a Hebrew inscription above the Ark. The inscription, the only overt verbal message in the building, contains the gilded Hebrew letters which mean: "Know before Whom you stand." Though this statement is somewhat paradoxical - one cannot fully know or understand God - there is an eternal emphasis on trying to know and attain a greater understanding of religion and one's position in relation to God.

Two of the most pronounced features of the main sanctuary of the Spanish and Portuguese Synagogue are the repetition of leaf and flower motifs and the cross-referential dialogue between the decorative arts and the architecture. The entablature of the building's facade contains intricately patterned designs and laurel wreaths. The pediment also has a laurel motif, and the Corinthian capitols display intricate carvings of vegetation. Flowers and wreaths of laurel are carved on the ceiling supports. The Ark which contains the scrolls of the Torah has a pediment with leaf and flower designs; its center contains a carved laurel wreath from which hangs the *Ner Tamid*, the perpetual lamp.

The candlesticks surrounding the reader's desk serve as a good example of the internal cross-referencing in the main sanctuary. Each brass candlestick represents a carved pedestal on which rests a fluted Ionic column. On top of the column is a goblet-shaped structure which holds a large gas-operated candle. These candlesticks refer to columns of architectural support; only here, they support the representation of a goblet and a light source. The candlesticks suggest a visual equation of physical supports with the support and elevation of the goblet and light. The goblet is a symbol of a ritual sanctification process, and light can be interpreted as spirit, knowledge, and transcendence. These images create a visual metaphor; the practice of the religion will, like a column, support our lives by giving us sanctity, light and spiritual fulfillment.

On either side of the Tebah, which holds these twelve candlesticks, are large Ionic marble columns that support the women's balcony. Though the predominant order of this building is Corinthian, the juxtaposition of Ionic columns with the candlesticks provides an interesting visual echo of references. Another issue of reference is the floorboards of the Tebah. A bit creaky, these floorboards date back to the floor of the reader's desk of the Mill Street Synagogue of 1730. The notion of walking in our ancestors' footsteps is made literal.

THE LITTLE SYNAGOGUE: A COLLECTION OF RITUAL OBJECTS

Also dating from 1730 are several objects found in the

Spanish and Portuguese Synagogue's smaller sanctuary known, for obvious reasons, as the Little Synagogue. The Tebah and its four surrounding candlesticks, some of the benches, and the Ten Commandments above the Ark, for example, have been in use since 1730. The Little Synagogue is used for daily morning and evening services, life-cycle events such as baby namings, *b'rith milahs* (circumcisions), and small weddings. It is currently also used for women's services and Megillah readings. Like the candlesticks in the main sanctuary, the candlesticks in the Little Synagogue have several references and layers of meaning. These candlesticks are designed with three sections, representing the three ritual objects involved in the *Habdallah* service, performed after sundown on Saturdays to bid farewell to the Sabbath and to usher in the new week. The objects involved are a candle (to show the separation between light and dark, similar to the separation between the weekdays and the Sabbath), sweet-smelling spices or herbs (to refresh one's soul in order to have a happy and productive week), and a cup of wine (to sanctify the separation of the Sabbath from the rest of the week). The candlesticks surrounding the Tebah represent a smaller candlestick, on top of which is a spice box, and finally, at the top is a wine goblet.

These candlesticks are sculpted representations of other ritual objects. They are objects with one function, yet they refer to another function. This clever interplay between function and transformation creates an aesthetic and ritualistic reference for the viewer, who can appreciate both the objects's function and its references.

Arthur Danto, in *The Transfiguration of the Commonplace*, discusses Aristotle's observation of the link between imitation, recognition, and pleasure. Danto notes that

> the knowledge that [the object] is an imitation must then be presupposed by the pleasure in question, or, correlatively, the knowledge that it is not real. So the pleasure in question has a certain cognitive dimension.

The candlesticks surrounding the reader's desks in both the main sanctuary and the Little Synagogue imitate things that they are not. This results in a visual play which involves cognition and recognition in order to get maximum aesthetic pleasure from these objects.

In the Little Synagogue are many ritual objects of historic and aesthetic value. On the wall opposite the Ark hangs a Sabbath Lamp of the Seven Wicks (1730). Hanging on the north wall are two bronze memorial lamps: one (dedicated in 1860, originally as a perpetual lamp) is decorated with flowers and wreaths, and the other (dedicated in 1925) has leaves and Stars of David carved around it. These ritual lamps relate to issues of memory in a religious and cultural context. The fourth commandment, "Remember the Sabbath," suggests the strong link between memory and ritual. The Sabbath is begun with the lighting of candles; the Sabbath Lamp of the Seven Wicks reminds the viewer of the six periods in the Creation and the seventh period of rest (Genesis I). This lamp is used to signify the importance of religious memory. The memorial lamps, on the other hand, serve to preserve cultural and familial memory. These lamps are lit on the anniversary of the deaths of congregants' relatives. A lit memorial lamp in the context of a synagogue conveys the image of continuity of the generations and the communal respect for those who have died. The presence of these different types of lamps brings collective memory and personal memory into the same space.

But the ritual objects in the Little Synagogue do not only preserve the memory of religious commandments and the memory of individuals in the congregation. They also preserve the collective memory of Shearith Israel's origin. Because of the combination of objects and furniture pieces from past synagogue buildings (in addition to the newer objects and windows), the Little Synagogue is like a photo album which can be entered. Each object refers to a different time period in the history of the synagogue, documenting the ties to ritual tradition and the continuity of a community.

RITUAL OBJECTS OF SHEARITH ISRAEL

Unlike the ritual objects in museums, the decorative arts of the Spanish and Portuguese Synagogue,

> some of which are of high historic and artistic value, are not static museum pieces. They are in use continually bespeaking a religion that is living, that is lovely and is loved, and that responds to the call of the Psalmist "Worship the Lord in the beauty of holiness."[7]

These objects are not on pedestals with labels next to them; their artistic value is very much linked to their function within a sacred realm. The interconnection between aesthetic beauty and religion is a universal trait of ritual objects. The visual pleasure of religious objects is at once awesome and comforting to the eye; religion is too large to understand, yet its aesthetically pleasing ritual objects can serve to concretize awe.

After Moses led the people of Israel through the Red Sea, he proclaimed: "This is my God, and I shall make beauty for Him" (Exodus 15:1). Rabbis have asked how one can possibly make beauty for the Source of all beauty. They answer: by fulfilling the commandments in the most beautiful way possible. The aesthetic considerations of worship date from biblical times. In this tradition, ceremonial and ritual objects were donated to and purchased by the community to create visually beautiful services and rituals.

Partial-showing in the aesthetic realm is a trait that crosses time and culture. It is evident in the rituals of the Spanish and Portuguese Synagogue. Like the Nazca lines in Peru which cannot fully be seen from a human perspective, or the art work on roofs of cathedrals, one generally cannot see fully every part of the main sanctuary of the Spanish and Portuguese Synagogue. The architecture, though rectangular and clear, has blocking elements in it; the balcony blocks the view directly above or below a person; the reader's desk can block horizontal vision. Though there are no pillars that interrupt the architectural sweep of the building, one can never see without obstruction unless one stands at the reader's desk. Here there is an aesthetic hierarchy; full clarity of vision can only be achieved from the most important point in the sanctuary.

The Torah scrolls are normally hidden behind the doors of the Ark. Even when the Ark is open, the scrolls themselves are covered with silk robes and adorned with silver "bells." The Torah scrolls are invocational objects which are only taken into public viewing at specific times. This partial-showing gives the Torahs aesthetic and ritual power; they become, in their hiddenness, a metaphor of sacredness, and in their display to believers in the Torah, a literal display of sacredness.

In addition to partial-showing, visual indicators in the rituals include the silk cloaks of the Torah scrolls. The color of the cloaks serves as a cue as to the mood of the day. On regular Sabbaths, the Torahs are clothed in red brocade cloaks. On Festivals or special Sabbaths (such as a Sabbath that falls on a New Moon, or the anniversary of the consecration of the synagogue), the Torah cloaks are multi-colored, a sign of festivity. On Tisha B'Ab, a day of national sadness, the Ark, reader's desk and candles are draped in black. Most striking are the Torahs during the High Holy Days, when all of the Torahs, the lining of the Ark, the pulpit, and the reader's desk are draped in white, emphasizing the purity and holiness associated with these days.

Certain bells are used only on specific occasions. The bells which were presented at the dedication of the 1730 Mill Street synagogue are used on the anniversary of the consecration of that synagogue. Anoher set of bells are replicas of the Liberty Bell. These bells are used on the Sabbath when the verse "You shall proclaim liberty throughout the land unto all its inhabitants" (Leviticus 25:10) is read from the Torah. Myer Myers crafted a set of bells for the synagogue, and these are used on the High Holy Days and other special occasions.

Aesthetic pleasure is very important in the ritual sphere. The ritual objects of the Spanish and Portuguese Synagogue, though, are not merely aesthetic objects. They also serve as visual cues for the viewer and participant; they have communicative value.

The history of the Spanish and Portuguese Synagogue as the first Jewish congregation in North America gives it an aura of authority and traditionalism. Its classical architecture reflects that authority, and ties the history of Shearith Israel to the long history of Jewish tradition. Its architecture and art objects make ritual practices aesthetically, as well as spiritually, fulfilling.

NOTES

1. Maurice Berger, "Arnold Brunner's Spanish and Portuguese Synagogue: Issues of Reform and Reaffirmation in Late Nineteenth-Century America," *Arts Magazine* vol. 54 n. 6, Feb. 1980,pp. 164-167.

2. Both of these synagogues were designed by Robert Mook.

3. Maurice Berger, p. 165. Page references in the text are from this article.

4. David and Tamar de Sola Pool, *An Old Faith in the New World*, Columbia University Press, New York, 1954, p.81.

5. The music of the synagogue, I think, is one area where antiquity and modernity meet; the choir sings both ancient melodies and choral compositions written by modern composers.

6. Arthur, Danto, *The Transfiguration of the Commonplace*, Harvard University Press, Cambridge, 1981,p.14.

7. David and Tamar de Sola Pool, *An Old Faith in the New World*, p.92.

SECTION TWO

THE UNIVERSALISTIC VISION OF JUDAISM

by Marc D. Angel

At the Revelation at Sinai, God chose the people of Israel to receive the Torah. This unique and unprecedented covenant between God and a group of human beings was to have an immense influence on human civilization. The Torah prescribed a specific way of life for the Jewish people. Yet, the Revelation-though aimed directly at Israel-was also concerned with humanity as a whole.

A fascinating Midrash points out that at the Revelation the voice of God divided into seventy languages, representing the seventy nations of the world i.e. all of humanity. The Torah, while containing a particular message for the people of Israel, also includes a universal message for all people.

Paul Johnson, in his *History of the Jews*, has noted that "the world without the Jews would have been a radically different place.... To them we owe the idea of equality before the law, both divine and human; of the sanctity of life and the dignity of the human person; of the individual conscience and so of personal redemption; of the collective conscience and so of social responsibility; of peace as an abstract ideal and love as a foundation of justice, and many other items which constitute the basic moral furniture of the human mind. Without the Jews it might have been a much emptier place."

The Jewish enterprise, then, has been both particularistic and universalistic. The Torah and rabbinic tradition have been the guiding forces animating Jewish life over the millenia. The halakhah-Jewish law-has been understood by the Jewish people as a Divinely-bestowed way of life. Through living a life of righteousness based on Torah and halakhah, Jews thereby serve as "a light unto the nations". The achievement of this ideal is dependent upon faithfulness to the particular teachings of the Torah as well as a universalistic vision for the well-being of all humanity.

Maintaining this equilibrium is a basic desideratum of Judaism. Yet, this vital balance is threatened by various trends in modern Jewish life.

On the one hand are those who stress universalism, while playing down particularism as much as possible. They advocate Jewish ethics, but denigrate the need to fulfill the specific ritual commandments of the Torah. On the other hand are those who are devoted to the mitzvot and rituals, but who are very little involved with the world at large. They retreat into their own spiritual and physical ghettos, often trying to drive as many wedges as possible between themselves and the rest of society. Both of these approaches represent a deviation from the harmonious balance implicit in classic Judaism. Our ethical teachings are rooted in the mitzvot. An ethical unversalism outside the context of observance of the mitzvot is not true to the Jewish religious genius. Likewise, a parochial commitment to rituals-without a concomitant concern for universalistic ethics-is also an aberration. Judaism emptied of its particularistic mitzvot is hollow; Judaism robbed of its unversalistic vision is cult-like, rather than a world religion.

The current tendency within the traditionally-observant Jewish community has been towards greater particularism. This tendency manifests itself in the phenomenal growth of the haredi (right-wing) community, as well as its pervasive influence throughout contemporary Orthodox Jewish life. Religious self-sufficiency and spiritual isolationism are dominant themes in the right-wing Orthodox way of thinking. As Orthodoxy has turned more and more inward, the universalistic aspects of Judaism have been relegated to the periphery of religious consciousness.

(Prof. Menachem Kellner, "On Universalism and Particularism in Judaism," *Da'at* 36, 1996, pp v-xv, has noted that the struggle between universalism and particularism in Judaism has ancient roots. The tendency towards particularism within traditional circles has a long history.)

The turn inward within traditional Judaism may be the result of centuries of anti-Jewish persecution by non-Jewish religions and nations. In the face of vast hostility and cruelty committed against Jews, it was natural for Jews to turn inward. Moreover, those Jews who have been most identified with universalistic attitudes in modern times have also tended to be those who have moved away from traditional religious beliefs and observances. Thus, universalism has been identified with assimilation and loss of Jewish religious integrity.

While the tendency towards isolationism may be understandable from a historical and sociological perspective, nevertheless, it is a tendency which needs to be corrected. Vibrant religious Jewish life needs to look outward as well.

The Torah (Devarim 4:6-7) tells the Israelites to observe and fulfill the commandments: "For this is your wisdom and your understanding in the sight of the peoples, that, when they hear all these statutes shall say: 'surely this great nation is a wise and understanding people'; for what great nation is there that has God so near unto them, as the Lord our God is whenever we call upon Him?" Interestingly, the Torah is concerned that the Israelites be perceived in a positive light by the nations of the world. The medieval Italian commentator, Rabbi Obadia Seforno, comments on verse seven: "The reason it is appropriate to be concerned that you should be considered wise and understanding in the eyes of the nations is that God, may He be blessed, is close to us when we call upon Him. This shows that He chose us from all the nations. And if the nations should think that you are fools, it will be a desecration of God's Name, for they will say: 'This is God's people.'" Since the people of the world look upon the Jews as the bearers of God's Torah, the Israelites' behavior reflects back upon the Almighty. If the Israelites are righteous and wise, then they sanctify God's name; conversely, if they are foolish and unrighteous, they profane God's name. The Israelites, thus, are not given the option of living in isolation, without caring about the opinions of others. On the contrary, they need to see themselves as emissaries of the Almighty.

These passages in Devarim are cited by a great 19th century sage, Rabbi Eliyahu Hazan (*Taalumot Lev* 1:4). Rabbi Hazan had opened a school in Tripoli in which Jewish children were given instruction in religious topics, as well as in other subjects - including several languages. He pointed out that "it is the praise of our holy nation that the peoples will say that this is surely a wise and understanding great nation with righteous laws and statutes, who should live among them. And if the scattered Jewish people would not know or understand the language of the people (among whom they live), they would be-Heaven forbid-a laughing stock, a derision and a shame among the nations. And their great wisdom and broad knowledge would go to the grave in obsolescence."

In this responsum, Rabbi Hazan has articulated a Jewish legal concept: Torah law requires that Jews be perceived as a wise people. They are obligated to be understood by their non-Jewish neighbors. Although Jews have their own distinctive religious way of life, they nevertheless must interrelate constructively with the non-Jewish community. This can only be done through communication and some measure of interrelationship. But the Jewish responsibility to the non-Jewish world is not merely that of setting a good example of wisdom and righteousness. The Jewish tradition teaches a positive and active responsibility for all people. After all, all human beings are created in the image of God.

The Midrash, commenting on the Song of Songs (4:1) observes that the people of Israel offered 70 sacrifices in the holy Temple during the festival of Succoth. These sacrifices were offered by the Jewish people to seek atonement for all peoples, all the nations of the world (symbolized by the number 70). Praying for the well-being of all the nations is a powerful statement of concern and responsibility.

The Talmud (Gittin 61a) records the law that Jews are obligated to support the poor of the non-Jews along with the poor of the Jewish community. Moreover, Jews are obligated to visit the non-Jewish sick and to bury their dead. The Talmud specifies that these deeds of compassion and loving-kindness are to be done "because of the ways of peace." In order to maintain a harmonious society, people need to care for each other and to offer help to those in need. Rabbi Haim David Halevy, Sephardic Chief Rabbi of Tel Aviv, has pointed out that our responsibility towards Muslims and Christians (as well as all non-idolaters) does not stem from expedience, but rather from a firmly established ethical imperative (*Aseh Lekha Rav*, 9:30 and 9:33).

Jews are commanded to be constructive members of society. The Torah demands that we be righteous and compassionate, that we seek the well-being of all people. This responsibility is not confined merely to the broad category of social justice, but extends to the general upbuilding of human civilization as a whole. Rabbi Benzion Uziel (*Hegyonei Uziel*, Vol. 2, p. 98) discussed the classic concept of "*yishuvo shel olam*," responsibility to help in the upbuilding of human civilization. This involves practical society building, but also includes expanding human knowledge. Scientific research, for example, helps us gain a deeper appreciation of God's wisdom. And it also leads to technological discoveries which improve the quality of life. Working to improve the human condition is a Jewish religious imperative.

As noted earlier, the Jewish impact on human civilization has been vast. We have given the world many ideas and ideals. On the other hand, we have also learned from the non-Jewish world. And the Jewish people has been strengthened by non-Jews who have converted to Judaism. In the words of Rabbi Eliyahu Benamozegh (*Israel and Humanity*, trans. Maxwell Luria), "each proselyte in becoming converted has contributed his own impulses and personal sentiments to the Israelite heritage." Rabbi Benamozegh argued that "in order to achieve the concept of a universal Providence extending to all peoples and sanctioning the legitimate rights of each, men must cease to believe that the national or ethnic group is all that counts, that mankind has no significant existence apart from the nation or tribe...We should not be surprised that such has not been the case with Hebraism, which teaches that all mankind has the same origin and thus that a single Providence looks over all."

Victor Hugo observed that "narrow horizons beget stunted ideas." Classic Judaism has included an idealistic universalistic world-view. Judaism's horizons have been great; and it has begotten great ideas. The challenge to modern Jews is to remain faithful to their distinctive mitzvot while maintaining a universalistic ethical idealism.

JUDAISM AND THE VALUES OF MODERNITY

by Walter S. Wurzburger

Т he extent to which the Haredi community takes it for granted that exposure to modern values adversely affects one's commitment to Judaism, was driven home to me by a young *Ba'al Teshuvah*. Suffering from culture shock induced by his move from an American college to a traditional Yeshiva, he was advised by some friends to speak with me as a relatively "liberal" exponent of Orthodoxy. At the conclusion of a rather extensive conversation, I gave him some of my articles and invited him to resume our discussion at his convenience. When he returned about two weeks later, it was to inform me that, since in my writings I expressed myself in contemporary cultural categories, what I had to offer could not possibly qualify as authentic Judaism.

A short span of time within the atmosphere of his Yeshiva sufficed to persuade him that modern cultural values are the very antithesis of genuinely Jewish ideas and attitudes. One of the hallmarks of the Haredi community is the conviction that Judaism and modernity simply do not mix. It is therefore imperative that one avoid as much as possible the risk of contamination by the "idols of modernity," such as reliance on objective scholarship, adherence to democratic ideals or belief in human responsibility for socio-political conditions. Morever, it is claimed that the Jewish ideal of unconditional surrender to the will of God conflicts with the emphasis upon personal autonomy, even as the loyalty owed to community and tradition cannot be reconciled with the ethos of permissiveness and individualism that permeates contemporary society.

Against this background it is readily understandable why the Haredi community maintains that the more we manage to remove ourselves from contact with modern culture, the closer we come to Jewish ideals. The only justification for becoming acquainted with the ethos of modernity is a purely negative one. In order to combat viewpoints antagonistic to Torah values, we must first discover their weak points by acquiring some familiarity with them. After all, the Sages recommended in *Avot*, "know how to reply to the heretic."

To buttress its case, the right-wing Yeshiva world invokes the Holocaust as evidence of the bankruptcy of all of modern culture. Even in the most open-minded Haredi circles, involvement with modern culture is never treated as an intrinsic value, but at most, grudgingly tolerated as a necessary evil. Thus some Haredi yeshivot condone secular studies to the extent that they are necessary for successful professional or business careers. But while concessions are made in this directions, it is insisted that the inner life of religious Jews must be hermetically sealed off to guard against intrusion of non-Torah concepts and ideals.

It is my contention that this categorical rejection of modernity is totally unwarranted. I emphatically reject the notion that all ideas, values, and ideals which comprise the ethos of modernity be lumped together and branded as enemies of Jewish spirituality. Instead, I advocate a more selective approach.

I admit, of course, that many modern values are incompatible with Judaism. But we need not throw out the baby with the bathwater. There are a good many "secular" ideas and values which can make an important contribution to the quest for a superior Jewish religious existence. That a particular concept or value comes from the outside rather than from within the Jewish religious community is not *a priori* ground for its outright rejection. The Talmud already warns against committing this kind of "genetic fallacy," when it declares, "Don't believe a person who claims that there is no wisdom among non-Jews."

I am persuaded that total isolation from modern culture is by no means a boon to our spiritual development. On the contrary, the creation of intellectual ghettoes exacts a heavy toll from us, because it denies us the opportunity to enrich our spiritual life with precious insights that human intellectual and moral progress has made available.

There is ample evidence that the formulation and interpretation of Halakhic rules does not take place in a vacuum but must take cognizance of historic developments. Thus the author of *Maggid Mishneh* observed that the reason why the owner of abutting property must be given preference over other potential buyers is due to the fact that while the Torah cannot possibly contain specific rules for all possible contingencies, it includes the "elastic clause" that we do "what is right and proper." It was in response to this mandate that the Sages deemed it necessary to enact this particular law.

The Talmud refers to numerous enactments by the Sages which were designed to advance the "ways of peace" or promote *Tikkun Ha'olam* (enhancement of social conditions). That the readiness to respond to changing historic realities did not end with the Talmudic period is demonstrated by the vast number of *Takkanot Ha'kahal* that were enacted by various local Jewish communities. Especially far reaching was the ban pronounced on any man who divorces his wife without her consent. Morever, the very nature of the institution of marriage underwent a radical transformation when, although it represented a practice sanctioned by the Torah, polygamy was outlawed by Western Jewry. The changed attitude towards marriage probably also prompted Jewish communal authorities to discontinue the practice of insisting that a couple that has remained childless for ten years resort to divorce. Similarly, single males were no longer subjected to communal sanctions in order to compel them to get married.

More recently, challenged by the different climate of opinion prevailing in contemporary society, the Israeli Rabbinate found ways and means to invalidate marriages which violated modern standards of morality. Although clearly permitted by Biblical and Rabbinic law, they refused to sanction the institution of concubinage or to recognize the legitimacy of the betrothal of minor daughters by their fathers, a parental right recognized by Talmudic law. Among other bold measures, which the Israeli Rabbinate adopted out of the desire to accommodate contemporary moral notions, was the decision to permit women to serve as witnesses in court cases. In order to do so, they had to use considerable ingenuity to deal with Halakhic objections to the testimony of women.

I now turn to a different area to illustrate my thesis that modern values may actually enhance rather than diminish our spiritual stature. It has been claimed that democracy is not a Jewish ideal. Thus the late R. Meir Kahane time and again inveighed against the Jewish "assimilationists" who invoke secular democratic ideals, for which, he claimed, no support can be found either in the Torah or in Rabbinic literature. In view of the fact that the Torah explicitly sanctions the establishment of a monarchy, in his opinion, any concern for democratic values is an outright betrayal of authentic Jewish values.

It should however, be pointed out, that, according to a Talmudic opinion, the establishment of a monarchy is purely optional. R' Naftali Tzvi Yehudah Berlin showed that the language of the Torah text itself indicates that the consent of the people represents an absolutely indispensable precondition of the appointment of a monarch. Similarly, numerous Rabbinic statements also corroborate the thesis that authority may be legitimately exercised only if it derives from the consent of the governed.

There can be no doubt that the influence of the democratic ethos makes us more sensitive to the religio-ethical imperative of concerning ourselves with the dignity and sanctity due to every human person created in the image of God. The importance which contemporary society attaches to human autonomy, individuality and liberty reinforces and deepens our understanding of the wider implication of *Kevod Ha'beriot* (respect for others), as they relate to the reverence for the uniqueness of human individuality and to the need to refrain from violating it either by force or manipulation.

Some will be taken aback by my claim that modern values enable us to reach for higher levels of Jewish spirituality than were previously attainable. Usually, we hear only about the decline of piety in the course of history. The Talmud frequently contrasts the superiority of past generations with the inferiority of their descendants. But just as a modern graduate student in physics knows more about the subject than Isaac Newton, we may also look upon our moral knowledge as granted to dwarfs standing upon the shoulders of giants.

Maimonides definitely endorses the notion of intellectual and spiritual progress. This is why he asserted in his *Guide* that many laws of the Torah were necessary only because at the time of the exodus from Egypt the Israelites were not yet ready for a higher level of religiosity. Recently liberated slaves were still so primitive that they could not imagine a form of worship that dispensed with a sacrificial cult. Similarly, he contends that the Torah speaks only of material rewards, because at the time when the Torah was given our ancestors could not yet grasp the meaning of a purely spiritual reward. In Maimonides' opinion, it is only because divine laws are immutable that they retain their binding authority even if in a particular case their original raison d'etre has become obsolete.

Modern Jewish thinkers have also recognized the possibility of religious progress. Thus R. Samson R. Hirsch subscribed to the doctrine of an "inner revelation" which progressively yields novel important moral and spiritual insights. Whereas the provisions of the Sinaitic Revelation are impervious to the vicissitudes of time, the content of the "inner revelation" is not static but continuously unfolds itself. It was this belief that enabled him to author extravagant encomia in praise of the German poet Schiller, whom he extolled for magnificently expressing the spirit of the Enlightenment and thereby making an enormous contribution to the edification of humanity and the advancement of genuine spirituality.

Another articulate champion of the belief in religious

progress was Rav Kook, who coined the slogan, "let the new be sanctified." Whereas many traditional circles adopted the Hatam Sofer's approach and frowned upon any innovation in Jewish religious practice of life style, he believed that new insights garnered from modern culture and science, when drawn into the orbit of traditional Judaism and integrated within the framework of a Torah perspective, would enhance the religious quality of Jewish life. This led him to denounce what he branded "pusste Frumkeit" (a narrow-minded and rigid form of piety concerned only with externals) and to deplore the widespread tendency of the Orthodox community to concentrate exclusively on those ritual and ethical norms which are explicitly prescribed in the religious codes. Although he unequivocally demanded obedience to all Halakhic provisions, he felt that without adhering to what he called "natural ethics" (generally accepted ethical norms) it was impossible to satisfy the requirements of the "ethics of holiness," since the latter is not a substitute for the former, but its very presupposition.

Additional evidence for Rav Kook's optimism regarding humanity's capacity for moral progress can be found in his position on vegetarianism. He explained why the consumption of meat was permitted only after mankind's moral degeneration unleashed the Deluge. When mankind was in such a corrupt state that there was no respect for justice or the sanctity of the human personality, it made little sense to demand reverence for the life of animals. But when mankind will reach a higher level of ethical sensitivity, vegetarianism may once again become the norm.

One of the most influential voices raised in the Orthodox community in behalf of a positive attitude towards achievements wrought by the secular world was that of Rabbi Joseph B. Soloveitchik. He maintained that the Torah does not merely sanction but actually mandates human initiative to harness the forces of nature for the benefit of humankind. We are called upon to become co-creators with G-d in removing suffering and want and thus serve His partners in perfecting the universe. Because they enable us to fulfill this task, scientific and technological progress represent religious desiderata.

To be sure, there are within the Orthodox community important figures who limit religious significance to conformity with Halakhic norms and who therefore categorically object to the thesis presented here. Thus Isaiah Leibowitz maintained that Jewish piety consists exclusively of obedience to Halakhah. In his view, Judaism is completely indifferent to whatever subject matters are not within the purview of explicit, formal Halakhic regulation. Hence, the cultivation of ethical sentiments, religious feelings, nationalistic attitudes, or political values have nothing to do with Judaism. Similarly, the *Hazon Ish* contended that the validity of any idea, value or ideal can only be determined by Halakhah. But as I have shown in my *Ethics of Responsibility*, what is religiously relevant need not coincide with the area regulated by Halakhic norms. The very fact that many Haredi circles subscribe to the doctrine of *Da'at Torah* (the thesis that religious authority extends to issues which lie outside the scope of Halakhah) proves that they, too, do not identify religious propriety with obedience to Halakhic rulings. They follow in the footsteps of Nahmanides, who noted that one may meticulously abide by all the specific regulations of the Torah and yet remain a scoundrel. Significantly, Rav

Soloveitchik, for all his insistence that Judaism revolves around Halakhah and that any authentic Jewish philosophy must be formed within the matrix of Halakhah, nonetheless pointed out that observance of the Halakhah was merely a floor, not a ceiling.

In keeping with this approach, it is my conviction that because Jewish piety includes subjective attitudes and beliefs, some features of modern culture may also qualify as positive contributions to wholesome Jewish spirituality. They may sensitize us to various values which should be integrated within a world view that strives for the implementation of the ever-beckoning ideal that we become "a nation of priests and a holy people."

PRAISE THE LORD, ALL YOU NATIONS

A STUDY OF PSALM 117

by Hayyim Angel

Hallelu et H' kol goyim;
shabbehuhu kol ha-umim,
ki gavar alenu hasdo;
ve-emet H' le-olam.
Halleluyah.

Praise the Lord, all you nations;
extol Him, all you peoples,
for great is His steadfast love towards us;
the faithfulness of the Lord endures forever.
Hallelujah.

Psalm 117 is the shortest chapter in the Bible.[1] Consisting of only two verses, this succinct prayer is included in our Hallel liturgy, proclaimed on every festival by Jews around the world.

At first blush, this Psalm contains a message dear to all ardently committed Jews: not only are we concerned that our fellow Jews develop a powerful religious connection with our Creator, but we ultimately wish that all people of the world will recognize God as the Master of the Universe. "And the Lord shall be king over all the earth; in that day the Lord shall be one and His Name one" (Zech. 14:9).[2]

Yet, a difficulty arises in understanding our Psalm. Why should non-Jews praise God and recognize Him as the true Deity because He has been steadfastly good to Israel ("for great is His steadfast love towards *us*")? Why does the Psalmist employ such a seemingly nonessential reason to draw people closer to God?

In tracing and analyzing the various approaches of our commentators to these two verses, we will find a striking range of opinions, reflective of philosophical standpoints on broader issues. Specifically, one will be able to isolate different attitudes toward our relationship with the other nations of the world.

I. MIDRASHIC RESPONSES: MULTIPLE VOICES

Our question is raised first by the Gemara (Pesahim 118b):

"Praise the Lord, all you nations": Why should the nations of the world do this (Rashi: to praise God for His steadfast love towards us--*we* should praise Him for this reason)? Understand [the Psalm] this way: "Praise the Lord, all you nations"-for the great acts and wonders which God does for them [i.e., the nations]; how much more should we [Israel], for great is His steadfast love towards us.

The Gemara divides the Psalm into different voices. The first verse is indeed a call from the Psalmist to non-Jews to praise God. But the second verse suddenly has Israel introspectively realizing their own duty to recite Hallel in gratitude for their special relationship with their Creator.[3]

In Midrash Shoher Tov 117:2, we find a similar line of reasoning, that our Psalm also addresses Israel's relationship with God. But this Midrash explicitly breaks our Psalm into three different voices, instead of only two:

> R. Shimon, son of our Holy Rabbi asked his father, "who are the 'nations,' and who are the 'peoples?'" (i.e., the verse appears redundant). He replied, "'all you nations' refers to those nations who have enslaved Israel; 'all you peoples' refers to those peoples who did not enslave them. The [latter] peoples said, if those nations who enslaved Israel are praising God, how much more must we, who have not enslaved Israel...
>
> [Upon hearing this,] Israel said, [if so,] we should praise God even more! They began to say 'for great is His steadfast love towards us.'"

First, the nations who have oppressed Israel (*goyim*) praise God. This leads those nations more benevolent to Israel (*ha-ummim*) to join in the praises. Finally, Israel (*ki gavar alenu hasdo*) recognizes God's unique relationship with them, and they realize how much more they are obliged to glorify God.

Although both rabbinic solutions may be viewed in the realm of *derash*, they poignantly illustrate how difficult our short Psalm is. We will now consider the *peshat* commentators, to see how they contend with our Psalm.

II. RASHI: A NEGATIVE PERCEPTION OF THE NATIONS' ATTITUDE TOWARD ISRAEL

Rashi takes a curious position regarding the other nations' respect for Israel. "Praise the Lord...*even though* great is His steadfast love towards us [Israel]." By adding a simple "even though" (*ve-af ki*) to the verse, Rashi has put a different spin on this Psalm. There are at least two ways to understand Rashi's gloss: 1) Rashi assumes that the nations addressed in this Psalm are distraught whenever Jews are crowned with success. 2) Even if the nations are not disturbed by the success of the Jews *per se*, they might be envious that God gives Israel special attention.

In either case, Rashi appears to intimate that the nations are generally unhappy about God's distinctive relationship with Israel. The Psalmist, whose vision is for all the people of the world to recognize God and praise Him, addresses this negative outlook towards Israel, and calls to the nations to rise above their initial hostilities, shifting the focus to God Himself.

III. RADAK: ANTICIPATING MESSIANIC TIMES

Radak[4] takes an approach different from Rashi: This Psalm speaks of Messianic times, when all nations will embrace God as their Creator, and will praise Him.[5] Radak writes that in the future, non-Jews will praise God, because they see how unfailing He has been in fulfilling His pledge of beneficence to Israel. Until that point, they found it difficult to believe in God's existence, since it appeared that Israel was suffering. When they see Israel's redemption, the nations will be so impressed that they will naturally gravitate towards serving God.

Rashi and Radak are not necessarily inconsistent in their understanding of the attitude of the nations towards Israel. Rashi asserts that the Psalmist is addressing the nations *now*, whereas Radak believes that the Psalmist is stating a prophetic vision of what things will be like in *Messianic times*. The primary argument between these two commentaries, then, is over whether this Psalm addresses the present or whether it prophesies for the future. The conflict between understanding a Psalm as a prophecy or as a prayer is a broad exegetical topic, running throughout traditional exegesis on the Psalms.[6]

IV. AMOS HAKHAM: *KIDDUSH HASHEM*
AND *HILLUL HASHEM*

Amos Hakham (*Da'at Mikra*) offers a straightforward interpretation of our Psalm. Throughout the Bible, we find the theme of Israel wishing that the nations will also serve God. However, it is easier to see the hand of God when righteous people are physically successful. When righteous people suffer, many deny God's Providence.[7] Hakham cites Psa. 115:1-2, which describes the opposite phenomenon of our Psalm:

> Not to us, O Lord, not to us but to Your Name bring glory for the sake of Your love and Your faithfulness. Let the nations not say, "Where, now, is their God?"

In contrast, Psa. 66:8-9 is philosophically similar to our Psalm:

> O peoples, bless our God, celebrate His praises; who has granted us life, and has not let our feet slip.

Hakham also cites Ezek. 36:22-23:

> Thus said the Lord God: Not for your sake will I act, O House of Israel, but for my holy Name, which you have caused to be profaned among the nations to which you have come. I will sanctify My great Name which has been profaned among the nations...And the nations shall know that I am the Lord...when I manifest My holiness before their eyes through you.[8]

Hakham argues that our Psalm should be taken literally:

the nations should praise God, because He has been good to Israel. Israel's thriving naturally will inspire the nations to pursue a closer association with God.

V. IBN EZRA AND MALBIM: PSALM LIMITED TO SPECIFIC HISTORICAL CONTEXT

Rashi, Radak, and Hakham, despite arguing over the fundamental nature of this Psalm, still agree that our Psalm addresses *all* nations. This point is supported by the fact that the Psalm solicits *kol goyim* and *kol ha-ummim* (*all* you nations, *all* you peoples). However, Ibn Ezra and Malbim explicate our Psalm in an historical context, understanding the Psalmist to be addressing specific nations, rather than all non-Jews.

Ibn Ezra attributes our Psalm to King David, who had vanquished significant regions of the Ancient Near East (see especially II Sam. 8). Addressing his new subjects, King David tells them to praise God. Ibn Ezra explains the phrase, "the faithfulness of the Lord endures forever" as a directive from King David for the nations to abandon their idolatrous beliefs and to espouse belief in the true God.

Although Ibn Ezra does not confront our question directly, it would appear that King David is entreating the nations in his jurisdiction to exalt God for two reasons: 1) Since God has allowed Israel to overthrow our adversaries, the defeated nations should acknowledge God's omnipotence. 2) Since their pagan deities are false, they should forsake them and praise God. The Psalm is a triumphant affirmation of God's dominion and greatness, which King David hopes will be realized by his former enemies.[9]

Like Ibn Ezra, Malbim also interprets our Psalm in an

historical context, addressing a specific group of non-Jews (as opposed to all nations). However, he asserts that this Psalm addresses the nations in the time of Sennacherib.[10] Sennacherib, during his great conquest of the Ancient Near East, exiled the Northern tribes of Israel, conquered many other lands, and repopulated countries with peoples of diverse backgrounds (see II Kings 17).

According to Malbim, our Psalm petitions specifically those non-Jews who were exiled along with the Israelites. When God liberates the Israelites who had been exiled, those non-Jews who had languished will benefit from Israel's redemption as well. Therefore, they should praise God for having been good to Israel, since they have gained themselves (albeit only through God's kindness to Israel).

To summarize the views presented thus far, Rashi, Radak, and Hakham maintain that our Psalm addresses all the nations of the world. Rashi believes that the Psalmist tells the otherwise reluctant nations to praise God, despite His having a special relationship with us. Radak avers that our Psalm foretells the Messianic age, a time when all non-Jews will praise God after recognizing His fidelity in His relationship with Israel. Hakham cites several biblical sources which affirm that when Israel is successful, the nations will naturally gravitate towards God. All three commentators understand *"kol goyim"* (all the nations) literally, referring to all non-Jews.

Ibn Ezra and Malbim believe that the nations in our Psalm are limited to specific populations, not all the nations of the world. Ibn Ezra asserts that King David is asking his subjects to submit to God's power, since God has helped Israel defeat the nations. Malbim contends that a later Psalmist addresses those nations who will benefit from Israel's redemption.

All five of these exegetes agree that in the phrase *"ki gavar alenu hasdo"* (for great is His steadfast love towards *us*), the "us" refers to Israel, and the love God has for us. The Gemara and Midrash Shoher Tov cited at the beginning of our essay also read our Psalm in this manner. But not all commentators concur on this point.

VI. R. MOSHE IBN GIKATILAH: A UNIVERSALIST INTERPRETATION

Rabbi Moshe ibn Gikatilah,[11] quoted by Ibn Ezra on this Psalm, asserts that God's steadfast love to "us" refers to the entire world (and not just Israel).[12]

> And R. Moshe says that it [the phrase, *kol goyim*] includes all nations. The meaning is that steadfast are the acts of lovingkindness which He does with *all*, keeping them alive and sustaining them.

It would appear, then, that R. Moshe would read the Psalm this way:

> *Praise the Lord, all you nations* (all nations, including Israel)...*for great is His steadfast love towards us* (all people, including Israel).

This universalist reading of our Psalm appears to be supported by Midrash Shoher Tov on Psalm 117:

> When a human king is praised, his supporters come, but his enemies do not. But everyone praises God, as it is written, "all nations whom You have made shall come and prostrate themselves before You, O Lord, and shall glorify Your Name" (Psa. 86:9).

> Someone asked R. Yehoshua b. Hananiah, "on what day is the

entire world equal, when all nations bow before God?" He replied, "...when the rains fall, all celebrate and extol God, as it is written, 'all nations whom You have made, etc.' When is this? 'For You are great, and do wondrous things' (Psa. 86:10). And 'wondrous things' refers to rain...for this reason, it is written 'Praise the Lord, all you nations'" (Psa. 117:1).

R. Tanhum says, "greater is rain than the giving of the Torah, for the Torah made [only] Israel happy, but rain brings joy to the entire world..."

This passage in Shoher Tov reflects the vision that all nations should serve God. The focus on the equality of all nations with Israel in praising God is made sharper by R. Tanhum, who considers rainfall even more important (at least in certain ways) than the giving of the Torah. Rainfall benefits all people (and animals), whereas the Torah is exclusively for Israel.

From this vantage point, our Psalm points to God's universal kindness to the world-and calls upon all nations (presumably including Israel) to sing to God for His largesse to "us," all humanity.

Perhaps the most fascinating aspect of this analysis is the fact that a Psalm of only two verses contains so much depth regarding a central aspect of our philosophy. When one realizes the profundity of the shortest chapter in the entire Bible, it gives one impetus to probe further into other sections as well.

NOTES

1. Radak begins his commentary by stressing, "this Psalm is composed of

only two verses." See Tosafot Pesahim 117a, s.v. *she-omedim*, which discusses different text variations for Psalms 134-135, rejecting one view on the grounds that "it is unlikely that the Psalm [i.e., 134] is of only two verses." Note that Tosafot does not challenge the length of our Psalm (117), leading one to assume that they had only one version, the one which we also have.

Meiri, on the other hand, includes Psalm 117 with its predecessor, considering them one longer Psalm.

2. See also, for example, Psa. 18:50; 66:8-9; 145:22; 150:6. In I Kings 8:41-43, King Solomon prays for the time when all nations will recognize God and come to the Temple which had just been completed and dedicated.

3. Abarbanel, in his *Zevah Pesah* commentary to the Haggadah, adopts a similar stance as this Gemara, but more on a *peshat* level. He asserts that Psalm 117 is addressed to non-Jews, telling them to praise God for what He has done for them. Abarbanel then understands the beginning of Psalm 118 to be Israel's introspective response to the nations' praising God: "Praise the Lord, for He is good, His steadfast love is eternal. Let Israel declare, "His steadfast love is eternal" (Psa. 118:1-2).

4. See also Metzudat David.

5. Many exegetes view this Psalm as referring to the Messianic era. See Meiri, Hirsch, Abarbanel (in his *Zevah Pesah* commentary to the Haggadah) and others. Radak and Metzudat David, however, address our particular question more directly than the others.

6. R. Sa'adya Ga'on takes an extreme position among traditional commetators, understanding all Psalms to be prophecies of David, not divinely inspired prayers (through *ru'ah ha-kodesh*). See Sotah 48b, which refers to David as a prophet. Rambam (*Guide* II:45) and many other later commentators assume that David composed Psalms while invested with *ru'ah ha-kodesh*, divine inspiration, but did not achieve the level of full prophecy.

Although most traditional exegetes assume that the Psalms are divinely inspired prayers, some remain uncomfortable attributing certain Psalms (such as 89, 126, and 137, which make overt references to the Babylonian Exile and the return from it) to authors living after King

David's time. They prefer to explain that earlier Psalmists composed the Psalms as prophetic visions of the exile and the subsequent return. See, for example, Rashi on Psa. 42:1. Ibn Ezra, R. Moshe ibn Gikatilah (quoted often by Ibn Ezra) and Malbim, however, ascribe several Psalms to inspired authors of later periods (i.e., from the time of the Babylonian exile).

For more information about authorship of the Psalms, see Bava Batra 14b-15a (which gives a listing of the ten authors of the Psalms); Shir ha-Shirim Rabbah 4:4 and Kohelet Rabbah 7:4 (which offer alternate listings of the ten authors of Psalms. Some versions include Ezra, one who could have composed those Psalms referring to the exile and return). See also Malbim's prefatory remarks to the Psalms.

For a thorough analysis of the exegetical positions of R. Sa'adya Ga'on, R. Moshe ibn Gikatilah, and Ibn Ezra, see Uriel Simon's *Four Approaches to the Book of Psalms: from Saadiah Gaon to Abraham Ibn Ezra*. Albany, 1991.

7. See, for example, Eccl. 8:10-11, "And here is another frustration: the fact that the sentence imposed for evil deeds is not executed swiftly, which is why men are emboldened to do evil." In contrast, Malkitzedek praises God upon seeing Abraham's success: "Blessed be Abram of God Most High, Creator of heaven and earth. And blessed be God Most High, Who has delivered your foes into your hand" (Gen. 14:19-20).

8. See also Psa. 98:1-4:

    Sing to the Lord a new song, for He has worked wonders... The Lord has manifested His victory, has displayed His triumph in the sight of the nations. He was mindful of His steadfast love and faithfulness toward the house of Israel; all the ends of the earth beheld the victory of our God. Raise a shout to the Lord, all the earth, break into joyous songs of praise!

9. In King David's famous Song of Victory (Psalm 18), he concludes with verses which support Ibn Ezra's theory:

    Exalted be God, my deliverer, the God who has vindicated me and made peoples subject to me, who rescued me from my enemies, who raised me clear of my adversaries, saved me from lawless men. For this I sing Your praise *among the nations,* Lord, and hymn Your Name (Psa. 18:47-50).

10. In both his introduction to Psalms as well as his commentary, Malbim

ascribes some of the Psalms to authors living after the time of King David, based on their content and/or superscriptions (e.g., Psalms 53, 89, 137). Later in his introduction, he also suggests the possibility that David may have prophetically composed the infrastructure for even these late-sounding Psalms, and a few saintly individuals transmitted them orally until the events happened. At this point, the righteous people revealed the Psalms to the public and recorded them for posterity. In the end, Malbim maintains that from a *peshat* point of view, one certainly may attribute certain Psalms to inspired authors living considerably later than King David.

Hence, from a *peshat* standpoint, Malbim maintains that Psalm 117 was written during or after the time of Sennacherib.

11. R. Moshe ibn Gikatilah was born in Cordoba at the beginning of the eleventh century, and lived in Saragossa and southern France at various points in his life. Rashi and Ibn Ezra quote from his works throughout their commentaries, usually referring to him as "R. Moshe," or "R. Moshe ha-Kohen."

Ibn Ezra refers to R. Moshe in his own book on grammar, *Moznayim*, as "the greatest of the grammarians," and "one of the great commentators." For a thorough treatment of R. Moshe's commentary on Psalms, see Uriel Simon's book, chapter 3.

12. See also Hirsch, who adopts a similar position.

MAIMONIDES' COMMENTARY

ON MISHNAH HAGIGAH II.1

TRANSLATION AND COMMENTARY

by Menachem Kellner

Sephardic Jewry in general, and Congregation Shearith Israel in particular, through its long line of distinguished rabbis, has been noteworthy for the attempt to integrate the culture of the broader world into the orbit of Judaism. Moses Maimonides, the Rambam, is the greatest adherent of this approach in the history of Judaism. His commentary on the Mishnah contains a brief passage, here translated into English for the first time, in which his position on the need to integrate Torah and Science is clearly presented. The passage is found in the commentary to Tractate Hagigah. Taking a text which was a *locus classicus* for mystical discussions in Tannaitic sources, Maimonides interprets it such that the study of physics and metaphysics (the sciences *par excellence* in his day) are presented by the Mishnah as being the ideological substrate for the fulfillment of the commandments of the Torah. I offer this annotated translation of the text as a mark of my affection and esteem for Shearith Israel and in particular for the distinguished incumbent in its pulpit, Rabbi Dr. Marc Angel, a worthy upholder of Maimonidean ideals.

MISHNAH HAGIGAH II.1:

One does not expound upon forbidden sexual relations in the presence of three, nor upon *ma'aseh bereshit* in the presence of two, nor upon the *merkavah* in the presence of one, unless that one were wise and understood upon his own. All who look upon four things, it were better had they not come into the world: what is above, what is below, what is in front, and what is behind. All who are not protective of the honor of their master, it were better had they not come into the world.

MAIMONIDES' COMMENTARY:[1]

He[2] said that it is forbidden to expound upon the "secrets of forbidden sexual relations"[3] unless those listening be fewer than three, the reason for this being that were one of them to engage the teacher in discussion, the other two could engage in discussion between them, lose their concentration [on what the teacher taught] and thus not know the correct law concerning the "secrets of forbidden sexual relations." Given the great desire most humans have for this matter,[4] they will not be sufficiently rigorous if a doubt should arise concerning what they heard from the teacher and they will decide the matter leniently.

He said, "nor upon *ma'aseh bereshit*[5] in the presence of two" and certainly not if they be more.[6] They said: "For ask not of the days past [which were before thee, since the day that God created man upon the earth, and from one end of heaven unto the other, whether there hath been any such thing as this great thing is, or hath been heard like it? (Deut. 4:32)] - one asks, two do not ask."[7] We have already explained the reason for this in our Introduction to this composition.[8] It is that it is impossible for the masses to understand those matters, and they are [therefore] only transmitted from one individual to another with great care, for the masses understand very little of them.[9] When a fool hears them, his conviction[10] becomes undermined and he thinks that they contradict the truth, while they are [themselves, in reality] the truth.[11]

But one does not expound upon *ma'aseh merkavah*[12] at all, even to one individual unless he is, as it was said,[13] "wise and understood upon his own," i.e., that he arouses himself to understand these matters on his own and does not need to have them explained to him. Rather he is given a hint, and he draws proper inferences on his own. This is the meaning of their statement, "they teach him chapter headings," [*Hagigah* 13a] [by which they mean] that these matters include issues which are impressed upon the souls of perfected human beings, such that when they are explained in [straightforward] language or expressed in parables they lose their meaning and significance.[14]

Listen to what has become clear to me according to my understanding on the basis of which I have studied in the words of the Sages;[15] it is that they call *ma'aseh bereshit* the natural science and inquiry into the beginning of creation.[16] By *ma'aseh merkavah* they mean the divine science,[17] it being speech on the generality of existence[18] and on the existence of the Creator,[19] His knowledge,[20] His attributes,[21] that all created things must necessarily have come from Him, the angels,[22] the soul, the intellect which links with humans,[23] and existence after death.[24] Because of the importance of these two sciences, the natural and the divine[25] -and they were justly considered important[26]- they[27] warned against teaching them as the mathematical sciences are taught.[28] It is known that each person by nature desires all the sciences,[29] whether he be an ignoramus or a sage. [It is further known] that it is impossible for a person to begin the study of these sciences, and direct his thought towards them, without the appropriate premises, and without entering the stages of science; they therefore forbade this and warned against it.[30] They sought to frighten one who directed his thought towards "the account of the beginning" without [appropriate] premises, as he said, "all who look upon four things. . ." They [also] sought to restrain one who would direct his thought towards and would examine divine matters with his unaided imagination, without ascending the rungs of the sciences and said, [with reference to such people,] "all who are not protective of the honor of their master [it were better had they not come into the world]."

"It were better had they not come into the world" - its meaning is that such a person is removed from the ranks of humanity, and classifying him in one of the other species of animal would be better for existence[31] than his being a human because he wants to know something in an inappropriate manner and in a way that is unsuited to its nature, for only a person ignorant of the nature of existence would seek to imagine what is above or what is below.[32] When a man empty of all knowledge seeks to use his corrupt imagination in order to know what is above the heavens and below the earth,[33] and imagines [reaching] them to be like ascending to the attic of a house, and also, [to know] what was before the creation of the heavens, and what will be after they are no longer, he will certainly be brought to madness and desolation. Examine this wonderful expression, said with divine help, "all who are not protective of the honor of their master," the meaning of this being, all who are not protective of their intellects, for the intellect is the honor of God [*kevod ha-Shem*].[34] Since he does not know the value of this matter which was given him, he is abandoned into the hands of his desires, and becomes like an animal.[35] Thus, they said, "who is he who is not protective of the honor of his Master? -he who transgresses secretly" [*Hagigah* 16a; *Kiddushin* 40a]. They said elsewhere, "adulterers do not commit adultery until the spirit of madness enters them" [*Midrash Tanhuma* Naso, 5]. This is the truth, for while one craves any of the desires, the intellect is not perfected.[36]

This matter is brought up here since above he said "these are the bodies of Torah," and thus here he cited matters which are the principles of "the bodies of Torah."[37] The Talmud forbade teaching them publicly and expressly prohibited it and commanded that an individual teach them to himself and not pass them on to another and derived this [prohibition] from the parabolic statement of Solomon on this matter, "honey and milk are under thy tongue."[38]

NOTES

1. I use the text of R. Joseph Kafih, *Mishnah im Perush ha-Rambam* (Jerusalem, 1963), p. 376.

2. I.e., the author of this mishnah.

3. The term here is *sitrei arayot,* on which, see Moshe Idel, *"Sitrei Arayot* in Maimonides' Thought," S. Pines and Y. Yovel, eds., *Maimonides and Philosophy* (Dordrecht, 1986), 139-56.

4. I.e., to satisfy their sexual urge.

5. The description of the creation of the world at the beginning of Genesis.

6. I.e., one may teach *ma'aseh bereshit* to, at most, one student.

7. *Hagigah* 11b. Maimonides is citing the Talmudic explanation for the restriction against teaching *ma'aseh bereshit* to more than one student at a time: one person may ask concerning "the days past," not two people.

8. See Vol. 1, pp. 34ff in Rabbi Kafih's edition. For an English translation of this passage, see Fred Rosner, trans., *Commentary on the Mishnah: Introduction to the Mishnah and Commentary on Tractate Berachoth* (New York, 1975), 111.

9. Maimonides is notorious for his intellectualist elitism. For other examples, see "Laws of the Foundations of the Torah," IV.11, *Guide of the Perplexed* I, Introduction, p. 16, I.7 (p. 33), and III.18 (p. 475). (Citations from the *Guide of the Perplexed* are to the translation of Shlomo Pines [Chicago: University of Chicago Press, 1963].) This elitism is a consequence of Maimonides' acceptance of the Aristotelian definition of human beings as rational animals. All that is not rational in our make-up belongs to our animal natures; the less rational we are, the more animal-like we are, and the more rational, the more human. Further on this, see below, notes 24 and 36.

10. Rabbi Kafih translates *emunato,* "his faith" (perhaps because Maimonides is here speaking about simple people). The Arabic is a variant of *it'iqad,* which, when Maimonides translates himself from Arabic to Hebrew (as is the case with the first positive commandment in *Sefer ha-Mizvot* and the first *halakhah* in the *Mishneh Torah*), he renders as some variant of *da'at,* "knowledge" or "understanding". It is important to distinguish "knowledge" from "faith" in Maimonidean contexts. To know something for Maimonides is, as Aristotle taught, to know it with its causes, not simply to accept it on authority. For an important discussion of this, see Shalom Rosenberg, "The Concept of *Emunah* in Post-Maimonidean Jewish Philosophy," I. Twersky (ed.), *Studies in Medieval Jewish History and Literature* 2 (Cambridge: Harvard University Press, 1984): 273-308.

11. It was because of this that Maimonides was forced to write esoterically. On his esotericism see my "Reading Rambam: Approaches to the Interpretation of Maimonides," *Jewish History* 5 (1991): 73-93 and my *Maimonides on the "Decline of the Generations" and the Nature of Rabbinic Authority.* (Albany: SUNY Press, 1996), pp. 43 and 98.

12. The vision of the prophet Ezekiel at the beginning of the book of Ezekiel.

13. In the mishnah on which Maimonides is here commenting.

14. Full understanding of metaphysical matters, Maimonides seems to be saying here, cannot be achieved on the basis of straightforward discursive learning. There appears to be an intuitive element.

15. Noteworthy here is Maimonides' emphasis on what *he* understood in this matter: "clear to me," "*my* understanding," "I have studied;" these sorts of locutions are relatively rare in his writing, especially in halakhic texts such as the Commentary on the Mishnah.

16. *Ma'aseh bereshit* thus includes two topics: the science of physics (as exposited in the opening chapters of "Laws of the Foundations of the Torah") and analysis of the question of creation. This latter is the dangerous part of the subject. A person who studies the question of creation and who (mistakenly) becomes convinced that the world is uncreated will reject the Torah, as Maimonides explains in *Guide of the Perplexed* II.25.

17. *Al-'ilm al-ilahi* in Arabic. This is the standard Arabic term for metaphysics. Compare further Maimonides' early work "Logical Terms," chapter 14, and my *Maimonides on Judaism and the Jewish People* (Albany: SUNY Press, 1991), pp. 65-79.

18. By this I take Maimonides to mean "existence as such." This is the subject matter of metaphysics as classically defined by Aristotle: being *qua* being.

19. I.e., proofs for the existence of God. Maimonides discusses these in *Guide of the Perplexed* I.71-II.1.

20. I.e., the analysis of the nature of God's knowledge. See *Guide of the Perplexed* III.13-24.

21. I.e., the question of which attributes may be predicated of God. See *Guide of the Perplexed* I.51-60.

22. Which for Maimonides are the "separate intellects" of the neoplatonized Aristotelianism which Maimonides adopted. See "Laws of the Foundations of the Torah," chapter 2 and the seventh of Maimonides' "thirteen principles," in conjunction with "Logical Terms," chapter 14. The equivalence angel = separate intellect is made

explicitly in the *Guide of the Perplexed*. See I.49 (pp. 108-10), II.4 (p. 258), II.6 (p. 262), II.7 (p. 266), II.10 (p. 273), and II.12 (p. 280).

23. The Active Intellect, the last of the separate intellects, and the immediate source of prophecy. See *Guide of the Perplexed* II.4, II.36 (p. 369), and the discussion in my *Maimonides on Judaism and the Jewish People*, pp. 14-15 and 26-30.

24. I.e., the question of human immortality, life after death. This is not the place for an extended discussion of Maimonides' extremely intellectualist account of human immortality. Suffice it to say that for Maimonides the *sole* criterion for achieving a share in the world to come is intellectual perfection (after moral perfection, which, as noted above, is achieved by Jews through obedience to the commandments). For details, see my *Maimonides on Human Perfection* (Atlanta: Scholars Press [Brown Judaic Studies], 1990), pp. 1-5 and my *Maimonides on Judaism and the Jewish People*, pp. 29-32. In this passage here, Maimonides has just listed the main topics of metaphysics. It is extremely important to get clear on what is going here. Maimonides has just claimed that the Tannaim were masters of physics and metaphysics. That is not to say that Rabbi Akiba studied Aristotle or that the Greeks learned the sciences from the Jews (As Rabbi Judah Halevi claimed) or that the books *Physics* and *Metaphysics* were "stolen" from the Jews (as later commentators on the *Guide of the Perplexed* were to claim). Rather, Maimonides is claiming that there is only one truth: what the Sages called *ma'aseh bereshit* the Greeks called "physics" and what the Sages called *ma'aseh merkavah* the Greeks called "metaphysics." In other words, the Sages were "scientists" (in the sense that physics and metaphysics were sciences, *hokhmot*) or the Greek philosophers were theologians. As Maimonides makes clear here and in "Laws of Foundations of the Torah," I.1 the foundation of all religious belief and the most general axiom of all the sciences are equivalent, namely that God exists. On the issue raised in this note generally, see my discussion of Maimonides' understanding of the lost philosophical tradition of the Jews in my *Maimonides on the "Decline of the Generations"*, pp. 43-49 (and the sources cited there). For commentaries on the *Guide of the Perplexed* which refer to the original Jewish provenance of Aristotelian books, see my "The Conception of the Torah as a Deductive Science in Medieval Jewish Thought," *Revue des Études Juives* 146 (1987): 265-79. For the

interpretation of "Laws of the Foundations of the Torah," I.1, see R. Isaac Abravanel, *Rosh Amanah,* chapter 5, fourth objection.

25. I.e., physics and metaphysics

26. Note well: the Sages considered physics and metaphysics important.

27. I.e., the Tannaim whose views are cited in *Hagigah* II:1.

28. I.e., discursively, and to anyone who wishes to learn.

29. An obvious reference to the opening sentence of Aristotle's *Metaphysics*: "All humans by nature desire to know." Humans, after all, are rational animals; knowing is the activity unique to them. It is no surprise that truly human beings have a great desire for knowledge. Maimonides is here implicitly explaining why the Mishnah lumps together three apparently disparate matters: forbidden sexual relations, physics, metaphysics. All three are the objects of great desire and all three are dangerous, the former because it can lead to sin, the latter two because they can lead to confusion and rejection of the truth. It is worth noting that the verb *y-d-'* applies to both sexual relations on the one hand and knowledge on the other hand. Maimonides compares the desire to know God (the final end of the study of physics and metaphysics, and the whole point of undertaking such study) to the love of a woman in "Laws of Repentance," X.3. It is further worthy of note that in his commentary on Leviticus 18:25 Nahmanides mentions that two sins cause the land of Israel to vomit forth its inhabitants: sexual immorality and idolatry. Idolatry, for Maimonides, is a consequence of mistakes in metaphysics (for one example of many, see *Guide of the Perplexed* III.51, p. 620).

30. Maimonides is here talking about the need to study the sciences in the proper order. On this issue, see my "Gersonides on the Song of Songs and the Nature of Science," *Journal of Jewish Thought and Philosophy* 4 (1994): 1-21. Note well also Maimonides' letter to his student with which he opens the *Guide of the Perplexed,* pp. 3-4.

31. I.e., for the existing universe.

32. I.e., this person wants to attain knowledge the wrong way, via the imagination, which can only lead to harm. It would be better, therefore, were this person classified with the non-human animals; humans, after all, are distinguished by their intellects.

33. A reference to our mishnah.

34. The intellect is that by virtue of which we can be said to have been created in the image of God. For texts and discussion see my *Maimonides on Human Perfection*, pp. 1-5.

35. This can only be understood in the context of Maimonides' Aristotelian comprehension of human beings as "rational animals" - humans become such only to the extent that they actualize their intellectual potential to some degree or other. For details, see my *Maimonides on Judaism and the Jewish People*, pp. 9-16 and 23-24.

36. This should be understood in the light of Maimonides' stand that moral perfection is a prerequisite for intellectual perfection and that intellectual perfection is not like money in the bank (as Lenn Goodman once wisely observed to me); it is, rather, like vigor or "being in shape". To stay in shape, one must constantly exercise. It is like treading water: if you stop, you sink. Thus, Maimonides has a problem with the notion of a wicked philosopher. Further on the points raised in this note, see my *Maimonides on Human Perfection*, pp. 26-28. The passage here may be better understood if we note that adultery (a classic example of forbidden sexual liaisons [*arayot*]) is almost always performed secretly. One who abandons one's intellect will transgress. Maimonides is using the Hagigah/Kiddushin and Tanhuma passages to explain in another way why the Mishnah treats under one heading such seemingly disparate matters as forbidden sexual relations on the one hand with the study of physics and metaphysics on the other: perfecting one's moral character (for Jews, through the observance of the commandments [using sexual relations as an example], according to Maimonides) is a prerequisite for achieving intellectual perfection; maintaining a high level of intellectual perfection protects one from backsliding morally.

37. This is one of the most important passages in all of Maimonides' writings. He is referring to the end of Mishnah Hagigah I.8, the mishnah which immediately precedes the mishnah on which he is commenting here. There the text speaks of *gufei Torah*. For other examples of Maimonides' use of this term, see "Laws of Idolatry," II.5 and "Laws of the Sabbath," XII.8. Both in Maimonides and in the Talmud (Berakhot 63a, Shabbat 32b, Hagigah 10a and 11b, Keritot 5a, Hullin 60b, etc.) the term means "specific halakhot." Maimonides here explains why the Mishnah brings up *ma'aseh bereshit* and *ma'aseh merkavah*: having spoken of *gufei Torah*, the Mishnah then turns to

the principles (axioms) of the *gufei Torah*, i.e., physics and metaphysics. Note well: we are being taught here that what may be called the ideological substrate of all the specific commandments is the philosophical sciences of physics and metaphysics. Properly to fullfill the commandments, one must be an accomplished philosopher. This point and its significance was first noted by Isadore Twersky in his *Introduction to the Code of Maimonides* (New Haven: Yale University Press, 1980), p. 361. For discussion, see my *Dogma in Medieval Jewish Thought* (Oxford: Oxford University Press, 1986), pp. 38-42.

38. Song of Songs 4:11. On this, *Hagigah* 13a comments, "The things that are sweeter than honey and milk should be under they tongue," i.e., not taught expressly. We here see Maimonides hinting that the study of physics and metaphysics is as sweet as "honey and milk" and therefore very attractive, even to the unprepared.

GUILT FROM, GUILT TOWARDS

by Reuven Bulka

T he matter of guilt is not merely a legal category or literary fiction. For many, it is a dominant motif in life, for better or for worse, and usually for worse.

GUILT, SHAME, AND PAIN

What is guilt? Perhaps it is best to make a distinction between guilt and shame. Guilt relates more to the individual's own conscience; shame relates to an abstract or sometimes real social standard. One feels a sense of shame when one has violated the social standard. When other people are aware of this breach, one feels ashamed in the presence of those others. Guilt is the reaction that develops when one does something which the person feels he or she ought not to have done, or when one thinks something that one ought not to think.

In the legal sphere, one cannot be punished merely for having a bad thought. In real life, however, we sometimes do punish ourselves for what we think, sometimes for what we do, sometimes for what we think we would have liked to do but did not do, sometimes for no reason whatsoever.

GUILT AND JUDAISM

In the minds of many, there is an association between guilt

and Judaism. The precise reason for this association is elusive. There is much mythical literature about Jewish mothers inflicting guilt upon their children. There are some who believe that because Judaism contains a massive code of laws, there is therefore a concomitantly high degree of guilt.

In reality, the matter of guilt within Jewish society is not universal. Much depends on the geographic locale, as well as individual circumstances that are not indigenous to Jewish life per se, but indegenous to certain combinations of Jewish life and Jewish experience.

Thus, guilt is more likely to be an issue among Westernized folk, among those living within a nuclear rather than an extended family structure, and among those susceptible to survival guilt as part of the post holocaust trauma.

GUILT AND PUNISHMENT

It is true that the Torah is replete with a host of punishments for breach of the commandments; punishments for transgressing many of the laws, whether it be murder, desecration of the Shabbat, eating food which is prohibited, among others. But it would be a mistake to think that those codifications are intended to impose guilt. They are needed primarily to create a value structure.

For example, from the fact that the Torah considers cursing a parent as liable to the death penalty, one becomes aware that cursing a parent is considered a serious crime. It would be impossible for the Torah to grade the relative importance of every commandment, be it an affirmative or prohibitive commandment, by saying that this is important, that is not as important, that is more important. Instead, from the severity of the punishment one knows what is crucial and basic to life, and what, in certain extenuating circumstances, can be waived; or which affirmation, in an either-or situation, has priority.

The punishment is not in place for guilt related reasons, but to transmit a value structure. Certain punishments were hardly ever meted out, and all the punitive rules have been purely theoretical for the past 2000 years. The punishment should be viewed in a positive rather than in a negative way. One would like to think that Jewish life would be greatly enhanced if the punishment inventory in the Torah were viewed in this manner.

EARNED GUILT

Since guilt is so closely related to low self-esteem, it is important to realize that Judaism takes a positive view of the person. The very preamble to the reading of the primary treatise on Jewish Ethics, "Ethics of the Elders" (Pirkey Avot), asserts that all Israel has a share in the future world (Talmud, Sanhedrin 90a).

All are born with the assumption that they are good human beings, deserving eternality. They are not individuals who have to be saved, not individuals who are so afflicted with guilt that it is only by God's graces that they are rescued from perdition. Instead, they are individuals who are meritorious because they are God's creations. It is essential that this be fully integrated as a basic motif of life.

Guilt, if it is to be legitimate, must be earned guilt. One may commit wrong actions in life, since this comes with being human. If the guilt has been earned, then it should be confronted. If one has committed a wrong, whether it be stealing, insulting, berating, or not living up to a responsibility, one is obliged to make proper amends. For stealing, proper amends requires the return of the stolen item; for insult, one must ask forgiveness from the victim of the outburst. For failure to act, one should try to act now, or to compensate as well as possible for the previous deficiency.

FORGIVENESS EXERCISE

It is vital to have the capacity to ask forgiveness of others. At the same time, it is likewise vital to be forgiving towards others. Forgiveness is a two-way street.

Jewish tradition mandates a most interesting exercise before retiring every night. At the same time that one recites the Shema, the faith affirmation statement, before going to sleep, one is obliged to extend forgiveness to any individual who had wronged you during the day. This act of forgiving is pronounced not only on the Day of Atonement. It is pronounced every single day, as a culminating act before retiring (see Hertz, 1971, p. 997).

It is quite likely that the most forgiving individuals are also the most likely to be forgiven individuals. One who is inclined to absolve others of their guilt because of the recognition that the others may have erred, will likewise be conscious in a healthy way of one's own guilt, and will therefore confront it in a constructive manner.

IMPOSED GUILT

Aside from earned guilt, there is guilt which is imposed upon the individual. It is for this type of guilt that modern jargon has coined the phrase. "Don't lay this guilt trip upon me." Individuals in society do not enjoy others making them feel badly, and are quite discomfited when this happens.

There is the classic guilt trip imposition related of the mother who gives her son two ties for his birthday. The son goes out of his way to show his appreciation by wearing one of the ties when he goes to visit his mother. The mother's reaction when she sees her son is, "What is the matter, you did not like the other one!"

Some people have a unique capacity for making others feel badly because they have not lived up to your expectations of them. This is one of the most classical manifestations of guilt.

In confronting this type of guilt, the "victim" must ask whether the guilt being imposed is imposed fairly, or whether it is undeserved, and therefore should be rejected. A direct confrontation is exceedingly crucial if one is to come to grips with this type of guilt.

It should also be emphasized that there are certain instances when the psychological establishment, or at least certain therapists within the establishment, do precisely that which they would reject if others do it, namely imposing guilt on others. Normally they are in the position of trying to alleviate guilt feelings, and sometimes they do so by eliciting the guilt. But there are instances when the guilt is used in a way which is slightly less than fair. The following episode will develop this point.

FRANKL'S EXPERIENCE

Viktor Frankl relates the story of a doctor who came to him after two years of unsuccessfully trying various forms of therapy in search of peace of mind. He had lost his wife and could not come to grips with the loss. In utter desperation, he finally tried Dr. Frankl. Dr. Frankl undoubtedly took a number of sessions with the doctor, but these sessions followed a crucial confrontation, in which Dr. Frankl asked the doctor what would have happened if he had died first and his wife would have survived him. The doctor answered that this would have been an impossible task for his wife. She would never have been able to endure and survive his passing.

Dr. Frankl then asked rhetorically whether it would not be possible for the doctor to look at his wife's death as a form of sacrifice. She had died first in order to be spared the agony that would have confronted her had he died first. The doctor was now enduring the pain that was necessary in order to free the wife from an even greater pain. In this way, Dr. Frankl suggested that the doctor could look at his suffering in a positive rather than in a negative way. Having opened up a positive avenue in which to view his predicament, Dr. Frankl eventually was able to bring the doctor out of his despair (Frankl, 1968, pp. 15-16).

Frankl relates that a little while later, when he told this episode to a gathering of psychologists at a conference, one of them pounced upon him and insisted that the reason why the doctor could not come to grips with his grief for such a prolonged period was because he hated his wife all along (ibid., p. 16), and he wished that his wife were dead. He was now racked with the guilt feelings that he had brought on by his wish for her death.

BEING HUMAN

In modern parlance, the terminology which refers to guilt is usually "guilt feelings." May has spoken about this terminology, about how it projects the idea that the only guilt possible is the feeling of guilt, but that real guilt is a non-starter (May, Engel, & Ellenberger, 1958, p. 54).

However, there is a fundamental guilt in human life, aside from the guilt associated with direct actions which are deserving of guilt. This type of guilt may be referred to as ontological guilt.

Ontological guilt is that guilt which comes from not living up to one's potential. This is not judgmental guilt; it is a guilt which derives from the nature of our being. Ontological guilt, unlike neurotic guilt, is rooted in self-awareness. It is not morbid, or given to melancholy. It is a guilt that is rooted in human nature, and should be a positive reality, leading to humility, sensitivity and creativity.

Maslow's self-actualizers have the unique capacity of integrating the frailty of human life with the sins of human life, to accept this as part of the human condition and to transmute this in a positive way. The healthy individuals feel guilt about their own short-comings, and who is free of any shortcomings?

Healthy individuals may feel badly about the fact they are lazy, or that they may be prone to temperamental outbursts; about their own jealousy, that they may be envious of other peoples' successes and happy about other peoples' failures, or they may feel badly about habits that they would be better off without (Maslow, 1970,pp.155-157).

Anyone who denies that these matters are problems in their own life is probably indulging in self-delusion. Instead, it is best to assume that we have these short-comings, to realize that these short-comings are strongly related to the fact of being human. Therefore there is nothing wrong and much right in confronting this discrepancy between what one is and what one ought to be. The only caution that one need to maintain in this self-confrontation is that one not become neurotic in the desire to eliminate all those faults.

THE RIGHT TO BE GUILTY

Frankl, quoting from Max Scheler, refers to his comment about the idea that one has a right to be considered guilty and to be responsible. As soon as you eliminate from the individual the sense of guilt, you lame that person's will to change (Frankl, 1969, p. 74). This is obviously applicable to deserved guilt, and certainly to ontological guilt.

Frankl himself often remarks that it is our human privilege to become guilty, and our responsibility to overcome guilt. In a classic confrontation with the inmates of San Quentin Penitentiary, he told those inmates that they are human beings just as he is, and were as free to commit a crime, and also to become guilty. Now, however, Frankl insisted to them that they are responsible for overcoming the guilt by rising above it, by growing beyond themselves, by changing for the better (Frankl, 1984, pp. 149-150).

REPENTANCE

A Rabbi once advised his students to repent one day before their death. The students jumped at this directive and asked the Rabbi how they could know when they were going to die. To which the Rabbi responded that you really do not know, but that since you may die tomorrow, you should repent today, and therefore your entire life is spent in repentance (Talmud, Shabbat, 153a).

The Rabbi was addressing students in the academy. In all likelihood, these individuals were not guilty of any gross crimes. The matters from which they needed to repent were probably everyday occurrences that fall into the broad category of ontological guilt. The Rabbi admonished that by engaging in repentance, they would assure themselves of a better quality of life.

In the Talmud, this process is described as repentance. In today's parlance, it could just as well be placed under the broad rubric of self-improvement, or self-actualization. The terminologies are slightly different, but this should not result in placing too much weight on the terminologies, and thus jumping to wrong conclusions. Repentance in the ontological sense does not refer to the need unfairly to weigh individuals down with a responsibility that is beyond their own capacity. It is rather to make them aware of the positive opportunities that await them, and which can be realized only if they become sensitive to these opportunities.

ENJOYMENT

Some individuals may feel guilty about enjoying life. They may think that it is a total distortion of God's master plan, and are convinced that enjoying life is a sin. This, in the Judaic context, is absolutely ridiculous. In the Jerusalem Talmud (Kiddushin, 4:12) it is related that individuals, after death, will have to answer some basic questions in their ultimate confrontation. One of the primary questions they will have to answer is whether they have enjoyed all of the many things that God has placed before the individual to enjoy, and if they have not enjoyed these, then why not.

It is hard to believe that one of the questions in ultimate judgment will deal with an item such as enjoyment. The fact that it is so high on the ultimate agenda indicates how important it is for living a meaningful life. It points to the crucial notion that one is obliged to experience the world, not to remove the self from it.

For removal from this world, God could have done a better job, by not placing the individual in the world altogether. Additionally, the only way in which one can truly appreciate God's majesty is by recognizing and experiencing God's creation and enjoying God's bounty in a full and meaningful way.

POSSIBILITIES AND REALITIES

There is no individual who is free from fault, but this is part of being human. The greatness of the human being resides in the capacity to overcome those faults.

There is a classic story told of a Sage who was once asked how he would discern who is a truly pious individual. The Sage said that the procedure to discern this is quite simple. He would ask any number of individuals the following question - if you found a purse full of money and you knew from inside identification who the rightful owner is, but you were also aware that the rightful owner did not know that you had found it, and you could therefore keep the money without ever being found out, what would you do?

The person who says, "I would keep it," is wicked, not pious. The person who says, "No doubt about it, I would return the purse immediately," is a person of false piety. The person who says, "I know that if I found such a purse I would have a tremendous desire to keep it; I only hope and pray that I will have enough courage to overcome the desire, and return the purse to its rightful owner," is a truly righteous individual (see Bulka, 1978, p. 62).

The message of this insight is quite clear. The true human dynamic resides in wrestling with ourselves, with our natural tendencies. If the human being did not have the tendency to steal, the Torah would not enjoin stealing. Often the difference between an individual who succumbs to ethical compromise and the one who does not, is a matter of price. Some may have a lower price for which they will compromise their souls, others may have a higher price. Still others may be beyond corruption.

But the truly great individual realizes that corruptibility is always a possibility. The question the human being must ask is, "What attitude should I take to my propensities?" The challenge is to answer this question by taking the proper attitude, and thereby overwhelming the potentially destructive forces.

PERFECTIONISM

In Judaic legal terms, there is a rule that for a prohibition which is devoid of any action, one may not administer any corporal punishment (Talmud, Sanhedrin, 63b). Just for thinking about committing a crime, one cannot be held responsible.

It may be suggested as a further extension of this principle, that not only can a court not impose punishment for a thought which never resulted in any action; the individual should not impose punishment on the self either, and should not engage in self-flagellation for having harbored bad thoughts.

Often guilt is associated with the feeling that the individual should be perfect. But perfection is not for human beings, perfection is for angels. The human endeavor really does not gain any currency from placing perfect people on earth. There is no purpose for a humanity which is perfect, but there is great challenge for the individual who is placed on this earth, with positive and negative propensities, and who must, in free-willed decision, opt for the correct choice.

In theological terms, the one who feels guilty because of falling short of perfection is guilty of a much more serious offense. Such an individual should feel guilty about going around in human clothing when that individual actually behaves as God. This guilty feeling about not being perfect betrays a lamentable distortion of what life is all about.

The Talmud asserts that the strong individual is the one who is aware of personal tendencies, and overcomes them (Sukkah, 52a). This affirms that the true human being is one who is aware of frailties, and is able to transmute these frailties. More than that, the really strong individual is one who has reached this level of greatness, through having had a greater propensity for aberrant behavior.

One of the fundamental rules of Jewish ethics is related to the matter of perfection. This rule states: "It is not incumbent upon you to complete the work, yet you are not free to desist from it" (Talmud, Avot, 2:21). It is not incumbent upon any one to complete the work of life, to think that one can actually be complete and perfect. Yet the awareness of imperfection should not therefore result in total inaction. Rather, one should strive, within the confines of plausibility, to reach towards perfection in whatever manner possible. This is the balanced essence of the human endeavor.

HUMAN LIMITS

Guilt, it has been pointed out, is usually associated with low self-esteem. Often, this low self-esteem may be inculcated from childhood. Some people may have a susceptibility in this direction. Whatever the case, it can lead to a serious manifestation, to feeling depressed and low, even to the point of feeling guilty about the fact that one feels guilty. When one is resigned to feeling perpetually guilty, and feeling melancholy about it, the eventuality of suicide becomes a real possibility.

In many instances, individuals do not confront their guilt in a healthy manner, and instead try to escape from the guilt by taking to alcohol, or to drugs, or to other artificial props. These substances may accomplish, on the installment plan, what the suicide action achieves more dramatically and instantaneously.

Cognition is an important element in the matter of guilt. From a Judaic perspective, it is essential to emphasize that one is "not to consider the self as wicked" (Talmud, Avot, 2:18). The individual who looks upon the self as wicked may very likely engage in a behavior pattern which becomes a self-fulfilling prophecy. Then, having engaged in this self-fulfilling prophetic action, one may turn around and further destroy one's self image with the ready evidence of the actions that have just been committed.

One need take to heart this instructive statement not to consider the self as wicked. The individual has the freedom to choose, but the individual must realize that it will not always be possible fully to live up to responsibilities. This is what makes life so meaningful, so exciting and so challenging.

APPRECIATING OTHERS

"Do not judge another individual until you have reached that individual's position" (Talmud, Avot, 2:5). Effectively this maxim means that one can never be judgmental about others, because one will never reach the other individual's actual position. Being in that other individual's position necessitates having that individual's mind set, and having reached that individual's predicament in exactly the same set of circumstances. Since this can never really happen, the maxim is a kind way of saying that one should avoid pronouncing judgment on others, or imposing a sense of guilt upon others through an adverse judgment.

The famous Judaic principle, "love your neighbor as yourself" (Leviticus, 19:18) is more precisely translated as "love that which accrues to your neighbor as if it were your own" (see Hirsch, ad. loc.). What is it of others that we can so appreciate? It is the other individual's property, the other individual's dignity, the other individual's self-esteem.

This basic Judaic principle argues quite forcefully that one should avoid imposing judgmental categories upon others, and in the process inflicting unwarranted guilt feelings. Since it may be assumed that no one wants this to be done to their own selves, then this should not be done to others. If anything, there is a universal responsibility to instill a sense of self-esteem in others, a sense of worthwhileness, of being appreciated. This is the best way one can manifest love for others in a tangible and realistic manner.

INABILITY TO FEEL GUILTY

Aside from the matter of unwarranted guilt, or the imposing of guilt feelings, there is the other side of the coin, the inability to feel guilt. A psychopath is not able to feel guilty, is never able to feel remorse for actions taken. Hannah Arendt reports on the dialogue with an individual, following the liberation of the concentration camps, in which this individual, under suspicion of complicity, was asked the following question, and gave the following responses.

> Did you kill people in the camp? Yes. Did you poison them with gas? Yes. Did you bury them alive? It sometimes happened. Did you personally help kill people? Absolutely not, I was only paymaster in the camp. What did you think of what was going on? It was bad at first, but we got used to it. Did you know the Russians will hang you? Why should they? What have I done? (Arendt, in Smith, 1971, p. 262)

The tragic irony of the situation is that the individual could almost nonchalantly admit to the most heinous of crimes, but could deny any culpability for those actions. Arendt points out quite eloquently that the evil genius of Himmler was that he was able to take the family man, and transmute him into one uniquely capable of murder.

Himmler and his evil machine were able to convince the family man that in order to protect those whom he loved so much, he should be willing to go out and kill those who are allegedly trying to take away from him the capacity to protect and enjoy his family. In their rational minds, they could never have been convinced to do this, but now the Germans succeeded in transmuting their very sensitivity into an instrument of hate.

Arendt relates the story of an individual who came out of the camps and was given his release papers by someone whom he recognized as a former classmate. The released individual looked at the classmate with eyes that spoke the accusing question, "How could you do a thing like this?" He did not have to speak the question, the question spoke on its own. The response he received from his former classmate was that he was unemployed now for five years and right now they can do anything they want with me (Arendt, ibid, p. 265). They succeeded in rendering the population limp, with no feelings whatsoever, in a way that one could justify the most evil of breaches and have no sense of guilt for it.

CONFRONTING THE PAST

Having addressed the matter of guilt, however cursorily, in many dimensions, including those who impose guilt and those who receive it, as well as those who feel guilty, whether they feel so deservedly or undeservedly, it is useful to suggest a general approach to the fact of guilt when it invades the human consciousness.

The suggested dynamic is quite simple. It is based on an insightful comment in the Talmud, concerning the individual who repents out of joy, out of love, for whom this repentance transforms the previous breaches into positive fulfillment (Yoma, 86b).

The behavior dynamic suggested in this Talmudic statement is revealing. An individual who confronts a previous action and realizes that said action was contemptible, and, in honest and sober assessment, uses the breach as a prod urging on a more positive approach, has transmuted that sin into a fulfillment. The sin has been used as an instrument for future positive behavior.

Sometimes, an individual may perform a good deed, and is so impressed with the self because of that good deed that one is likely to absolve the self of many future responsibilities. With such a reaction, the commandment is invested with a negative energy. On the other hand, one can invest a transgression with a positive energy.

The Day of Atonement, the day in which the community as a whole and all individuals within the community are expected to confront their guilt, is known as Yom Kippur. Interestingly, the word "kippur," although usually translated as atonement, is more linked with the Hebrew word for covering over, not in the Watergate sense, but in the sense of overlaying, of covering matter with other material (see Genesis, 6:14).

The implication of this is that on the Day of Atonement we do not make the past breaches disappear, because what has once happened cannot be erased. But there is much that can be done. One can build upon the past, however contemptible, and overlay it with good deeds that smother the sin and transmute the sin into a fulfillment. In a word, one may glorify life by rising above circumstances; one may learn from the past to build for the future.

FROM AND TOWARDS

The Talmud suggests that instead of wallowing in the self pity that comes with suffering "guilt from," it is preferable to think along the lines of "guilt towards," of pointing the guilt to the future, and using the guilt as a directional compass for where one should go in the future.

This general approach is useful for individuals who are dealing with their own specific guilt ridden circumstances, and may even be a good underpinning for the clinical approach to guilt on a cognitive level.

It may be preferable, in confronting the guilt of an individual who feels badly about having had an abortion performed, to look for ways to learn from the guilt feeling in a positive manner. This may be in terms of adopting a child, or of becoming pregnant once again and carrying the child through to term.

The individual who feels guilty about not having done enough for a parent or another loved one who has just passed away, may have legitimate reasons for feeling this way. Instead of an approach which would try to absolve the individual from this guilt feeling, it may sometimes be more appropriate to confront the guilt, even though the guilt may not be deserved. What has passed cannot be brought back. Instead, knowing full well the deficiencies of the past, one can therefore be urged to go an extra mile with a surviving parent, or other loved ones. The approach would orient toward the future, rather than trying to explicate the past.

It is recognized that the situation involving guilt may be quite complex, and may necessitate some long-term therapeutic intervention. However, in certain clinical situations, and certainly on a meta-clinical level, the orientation to "guilt towards" as opposed to "guilt from," can be quite useful.

From all that has been said, it may be conjectured that guilt in and of itself is value neutral. Since guilt can be used in a positive manner, and also in a destructive manner, it is not the guilt itself, but what is done with it, that is crucial. It is the task of individuals confronted with guilt, or those in a position to help such individuals, to invest guilt with a positive thrust.

THE CHALLENGE OF MODERNITY
TO THE JEWISH PEOPLE:
RABBI JOSEPH B. SOLOVEITCHIK'S
COVENANTAL RESPONSE

by Howard Joseph

P rior to the advent of modernity, Jewish identity was rooted in a sense of being a self-governing separate nation, guiding itself in public and private life by the teachings of Torah while waiting for the Messiah to bring us from exile back to our own land. Modernity's twin engines of Emancipation and Enlightenment brought severe challenges in their wake. While we often construe these as being of a predominantly intellectual nature, a moment of reflection suggests otherwise. Modernity has challenged the notion of a Jewish nation with a unique and separate destiny no less than whatever questions to the theological and philosophical contents of traditional Judaism. In fact, looked at from the position of those who abandon Jewish life and practice, it is rarely the philosophical issues that bring about their defection. However, there is no doubt that the modern open and democratic society in which we live poses the greatest test to our traditional self-understanding. Are we in exile if we are members of the nation-states in which we live? Are we part of a Jewish nation if we are citizens of other nations? How is it possible to separate ourselves from the lifestyles of those among whom we intimately mix? Maintaining a strong and sustaining sense of Jewish distinctiveness for the majority of Jews is certainly more challenging than, for example, explaining the relation of science and Judaism to the minority of intellectuals who are bothered by their seeming contradictions.

The challenge to Jewish peoplehood is so demanding because it goes to the very foundation of the society in which we live so well. Participation in this society was conceived as being separate from any religious tests or identity. Religion would be officially irrelevant to membership in it. All would be welcome if they were to be loyal citizens of the centralized modern state that would guarantee the rights of liberty, equality and fraternity to all within its domain. No group would maintain any residual self-governing powers; there would be no state within a state. This was the expectation or the price of entry. Most Jews were willing to pay it. Integration into the life of the general society was considered by most observers to be an unmixed blessing.

Thus, the plan of Emancipation foresaw a disappearance of the national character of Judaism. This was made clear even by the advocates of Jewish integration. On December 23, 1789, Count Stanislas de Clermont-Tonnere rose in the French National Assembly to champion the cause of the Jews. His famous pronouncement embodied the train of thought of even the most fervent supporters of the Jews: "The Jews should be denied everything as a nation, but granted everything as individuals. They must be citizens.... there cannot be one nation within another nation.... Every one of them must individually become a citizen; if they do not want this, they must inform us and we shall be compelled to expel them. The existence of a nation within a nation is unacceptable to our country."[1] In brief, there is no room for national distinctiveness, autonomy and self-government within the new social-political construct that modernity brought into existence.[2]

Given this orientation it is no wonder that many Jews believed that the price must be paid. The alternative was to risk expulsion from countries that were promising tolerance and brotherhood. Integration was more desirable than the perpetual state of pariahship to which pre-modern Jews were consigned.

So modernity confronted the individual Jew with a demand to relinquish those aspects of Judaism which perpetuated national distinctiveness. There is room for Judaism as a religion among other religions in the modern state although some expected Judaism to disappear as a result of the process of integration. Others said Judaism must be refashioned or reformed into a proper religion similar to the other religions practiced in modern states. In this way Jews would be acceptable as normal citizens.

These concerns affected all branches of Judaism to one degree or another in the past 200 years. Debates and disputes about who we are and what we are have continuously erupted during this period. Are we a nation? A culture? A religion? A civilization? All of us remember these questions being of importance to us and our friends at some point in our lives.

This question seems to be a permanent item on the agenda of modern Jewry. At certain moments it was brought more sharply into focus than others. When Herzl called for the first Zionist Congress, German Jewry forced the meeting out of Germany by strong protests to the government. Herzl settled for Basle. During the Holocaust years American Jewry was overly shy in calling attention to the atrocities of Hitler. Was it out of concern to display Jewish national sentiments in public for fear of risking our security here? In 1947, when the United Nations debated the formation of the State of Israel we know too well that many Jews were uncomfortable and actively opposed the birth of the state, thank God to no avail. It was only in 1967 that American Jewry came out of the closet with its support for and identification with the State of Israel.

How then can we respond to modernity when it attempts to deny a fundamental sense of our being? How can we articulate the necessity of the national component of Jewish identity in such a way that is convincing to ourselves and to others who may be interested? For me the answer lies in the concept of covenant which is so familiar to us. But it is in the unique manner of understanding proposed by our late teacher and master, Rabbi Joseph Soloveitchik, z'l.

We are familiar with the concept of covenant. There is an Ancestral Covenant -Berit Abot- struck with the fathers and mothers of Israel that has sanctified the nation that is their descendants. We are a consecrated, holy people because of this covenant.

The early, Ancestral Covenant is followed by a covenant at Mt. Sinai when the redeemed from Egypt gathered to hear the Words. We can speak about this event as an expansion of the covenant. A bond that prevailed between God and a family was now expanded to include a whole nation.

However, as I will demonstrate, Rabbi Soloveitchik does not see the two covenants as necessarily excluding or superseding one another. They are both present in Jewish thinking over the ages and operate together to express the complete covenantal consciousness of the Jewish faith. We could call them the two foci of covenantal consciousness, or even, to borrow a phrase from Buber in a different context, the two foci of the Jewish soul. They are two separate structures.

THE ANCESTRAL COVENANT - BERIT ABOT

We Jews have always understood ourselves as being part of a covenant between our people and God which derives from our ancestors Abraham and Sarah, Isaac and Rebecca, Jacob and Rachel and Leah. We recall how God beckons to Abraham and Sarah from their native land. When they arrive in the land the Covenant is established: "I will maintain my covenant between Me and you, and your offspring to come, as an everlasting covenant throughout the ages, to be God to you and to your offspring to come. I give the land you sojourn in to you and your offspring to come, all the land of Canaan, as an everlasting possession. I will be their God" (Gen. 17/7-8). The designation and the sanctification of the people are eternal, inherited from generation to generation.

THE SINAI COVENANT - BERIT SINAI

There is a second covenant of importance for our purposes. The tone of this alliance is already hinted at in the Abraham cycle of stories. However, it does not emerge into full consciousness until Mt. Sinai. We read the following in Genesis in the prelude to the destruction of Sodom: "Shall I hide from Abraham what I am about to do, since Abraham is to become a great and populous nation and all the nations of the earth are to bless themselves by him? For I have singled him out, that he may instruct his children and his posterity to keep the way of the Lord by doing what is just and right, in order that the Lord may bring about for Abraham what has been promised him" (18/17-19).

Later, at Mt. Sinai, this intimation of 'keeping the way of the Lord' becomes the Torah, the pattern of 613 commandments that are to guide the life of Abraham's descendants, the newly liberated People of Israel.

Rabbi Soloveitchik understands that these two covenants continue to function together, the second not superseding the first. Thus, the people of Israel has a double covenantal sanctity: the Ancestral Covenant with its focus on the people and the land, and the Sinai Covenant with its focus on the commandments.

THE CONTENT OF THE COVENANTS

Rabbi Soloveitchik discussed these two covenants in a now famous address to the Religious Zionists of America, the Mizrachi, in the 1960's[3] He noted that the content of the Sinai covenant is clear to us. "It expresses itself in statutes and judgments, in the undertaking to observe 613 commandments." This gives the Jewish People its distinct character and purpose - its *yiud*. He then asked, "but what is the content of the Ancestral covenant? Apart from circumcision, God did not give commandments to the Ancestors.... It seems to me that the content of the Ancestral Covenant manifests itself in the sense of seclusion of the Jew; in existential isolation; in the struggle against secular philosophies and political forces which the cultured non-Jew ignores; in the fact that the security of society generally does not ipso facto provide security for the Jew. In other words, the Judaism of the Ancestral covenant is expressed in our identification with Abraham the Hebrew - "All the world on one side and he on the other." (This latter quotation is a Midrashic comment upon the Hebrew word - *Ibri*. The root *eber* can mean 'on the other side.')

"The Ancestral Covenant is realized within Jewish consciousness because others point and say: Jew! In a word, the Ancestral Covenant finds expression in the sense of oneness with Klal Yisrael, the entire collective of Israel, in one's participation in the lot of all Jews, and in the consciousness of the fact that being Jewish is singular and unique. One who lacks this mentality and does not sense oneself as bound to the strange, paradoxical Jewish fate, lacks the sanctity of the Ancestral Covenant. One may observe the Torah and commandments and be fully within the Covenant of Sinai, yet at the same time profane the Ancestral sanctity." In other words, this covenant is one of fate, destiny - *goral*.

The Rav illustrated this point with a remarkable story. "I first became aware of this sensational revelation when a famous German rabbi, fully observant, let slip the remark in my then young, naive and timorous presence that he had more in common with a German than he had with an irreligious Polish Jew. Certainly, he added, I am closer to R. Haim Ozer because the Shulhan Arukh binds us together, but what connection do I have to such a one?"

"I thought at the time that what he had in common with the non-religious Polish Jew was the fact that in the eyes of the Jew-hater they were both Jews, and that the Jew-hater would make no distinction between them.... Later, to our sorrow, many Western Jews discovered their kinship to Jews of other lands and other traits.... Unfortunately, that type of Jew, who rebels against the Ancestral Covenant, is emerging here also. True, this Jew is religious and careful to observe mitzvot, but does not have a Jewish fate consciousness."

Thus, we can say that from the Ancestral Covenant we derive our strong sense of family belonging and common destiny: we are the children of the fathers and mothers of Israel. As members of the same family we care for each other, rejoice in each others' successes, and cry when any segment of the family faces tragedy. On the other hand, the Sinai Covenant is one of learning and doing: specifically, to learn to do that which was commanded to us. The central figure in this mode is Moses, who is known in Jewish tradition as "our Teacher."

The Sinai Covenant is strengthened by study. How is the Ancestral Covenant maintained? While it is true that anti-semitism does remind us of our ancestral family identity, it is a negative force. We do not wish for its manifestation. R. Soloveitchik asks, then, "how can we remain conscious of the God of Abraham, our Ancestral sanctity, in the midst of quietude and wealth, freedom and repose?"

His answer is remarkable. "Providence has given us the answer through the State of Israel.... The very fact that Israel is isolated internationally, that the vast majority of Klal Yisrael is sympathetic towards her and ready to suffer all manner of charges against her by Jew-haters; the fact that we identify with the State and see all who oppose it as Jew-haters, the very fact that we know this is our problem which no outsider can understand, sanctifies us with the sanctity of the

Ancestors.... Take away Eretz Yisrael, and the Jews of the Diaspora will be engulfed by a tremendous wave of estrangement and assimilation. All the dramatic, tragic experience of the sanctity of the Ancestors, the existential difference in Jewish history, would, far be it, wiped out. And who could say that we would be able to save the sanctity of Sinai if the Jew ceased to feel the Ancestral sanctity in its full tragic depth.... To save the covenant of their ancestors at Sinai, I must realize the Ancestral Covenant..., that is, to be at one with the suffering and joy of Klal Yisrael." Finally, Rabbi Soloveitchik affirms, "We recognize that the State of Israel is an instrument in the hands of God for the dual remembering, the one the Ancestral Covenant, the other, the Sinai Covenant."

Thus, for Rabbi Soloveitchik both covenants persist. The Ancestral Covenant has not been absorbed nor transcended. It remains a critical part of Jewish consciousness, bringing with it its own concerns and dynamics.

THE COVENANT AND THE LAND

For example, the Ancestral Covenant is always linked to the promise of the land of our people. In fact, one could say that the fulfillment of the Ancestral Covenant depends upon our possession of the land. From the beginning this relationship included the Land of Israel as an indispensable constituent of the covenantal reality. Their God who beckons to Abraham and Sarah from their native land was 'Elohei Ha-aretz,' the God of the Land. As we have seen above, when Abraham and Sarah arrive in the land the Covenant is established: "I will maintain my covenant between Me and you, and your offspring to come, as an everlasting covenant throughout the ages, to be God to you and to your offspring to come. I give the land you sojourn in to you and your offspring to come, all the land of Canaan, as an everlasting possession. I will be their God" (Gen. 17/7-8). The designation and the sanctification of the people are inseparable from the sanctity of the land.

The promise to Abraham and Sarah was confirmed to the descendant ancestors. Later, when Moses is sent to Egypt to deliver the people from bondage, it is in the name of the Ancestral Covenant that he labors. There is only one destination possible after the Exodus: the land of Israel.

Upon entering the land under the leadership of Joshua he is charged: "Be strong and resolute, for you shall apportion to this people the land that I swore to their ancestors to give them" (Jos. 1/6).

After taking possession of the land, the Israelite farmer was to come with his tithe to the Sanctuary. As part of the Tithe Confession he was to offer the following prayer: Look down from your holy abode, from heaven, and bless your people Israel and the soil You have given us, a land flowing with milk and honey, as You swore to our ancestors" (Deut. 26/15).

The references are too numerous to recite. What they all indicate is an inseparable bond between our people and the land, between Holy People and Holy Land. The destinies of our people and this land are linked, bound together by God's promise. Whether in the land or in exile, it remains part of our identity and consciousness.

Thus, as we have seen, the people of Israel has a double covenantal sanctity: the holiness of the Ancestral Covenant with its promise of the land and the holiness of the Sinai

Covenant with its commandments. From the perspective of the first, Israel abroad, out of its land is incomplete. It is not fulfilling its duty to settle the land and dwell in it as God's people; its sanctity is diminished.

MESSIANIC-REDEMPTIVE IMPLICATIONS

Each of the covenants has its own redemptive dynamic. For the Berit Abot the drama of redemption is focused on the land. Away from the land, Israel is incomplete, in exile, the covenant remaining unfulfilled. The return to the land, therefore, has Messianic significance. The covenant is actualized: once again the God of the land is their God. Possession of and sovereignty over the land is the sign of return to redemptive favor, possibly the beginning of a Messianic era. No wonder the sparks of Messianic fervor have repeatedly flared up since 1948.

The Sinai covenantal consciousness is concerned for the actualization of its program of Torah commandments as the guiding force of every phase of the life of the people. It is focused on the question of Jews having the power to create the circumstances in which to implement the covenantal terms. Return to the land may be a sign of forgiveness for whatever failings caused the people to go into exile and is for the purpose of a new opportunity to improve upon past performance. Hopefully, the more perfected Torah-inspired society will result.

The religious significance of the Land of Israel for Jews involves both covenants. They work in tandem and produce different emphases. They even exist in religious and secularized forms. Thus, in the development of Zionism, we find religious Jews as well as secular Zionists concerned for the survival of the Jewish people. They feared that the Emancipation and its aftermath would lead either to total assimilation or antisemitic annihilation. Their anticipations were unfortunately realized and confirmed in the Holocaust as well as the general assimilation that pervades Diaspora communities.

We also find religious Zionists who are motivated by the Sinai concerns, the opportunity to fulfill more of the covenantal responsibilities in the land than outside of it, including the command to settle the land and make it thrive. Secular Zionists also have a version of the Sinai consciousness: they wish to build a society rooted in Jewish values of justice.

The Zionist enterprise has been motivated by both forms of covenantal consciousness. The Berit Abot was in danger. Soon the Berit Sinai would be threatened as well, as the process of indigenization proceeded in modern society. Jewish sovereignty in the ancient Jewish homeland was a necessity for the survival of both covenantal impulses. A strong nation-state would be the guarantor of the physical survival and spiritual renewal of the Jewish people everywhere.

IMPLICATIONS

Through his understanding of the covenantal theology of the Torah, Rabbi Soloveitchik has firmly established the particular national identity of the Jewish people: it is covenantal, grounded in the relationship between ourselves and God. Our nationhood is not like that of others that existed for centuries or emerged under the pressure of modern history. If we take Torah seriously, we must treat our nationhood seriously as well. It is an inseparable component of one system. Those who suggest otherwise, Jew or not, have no appreciation of the fundamentals of Judaism.

Focusing on the Ancestral Covenant has other implications for our theme. Thus, the rebirth of the State of Israel in our ancestral covenanted land has signalled a renewed commitment to Jewish peoplehood which has always been the essence of the Ancestral Covenant consciousness. In that perspective, the survival of our people through history is itself a sacred phenomenon, inspiring many Jews today - committed Jews as well as those somewhat alienated from tradition - to strengthen their Jewish attachments and even deepen their understanding of the religious, spiritual and moral teachings that constitute our heritage and are derived from the Sinai Covenant.

Those who appreciate the Ancestral Covenant do not isolate themselves from other Jews. Whether or not they recognize or fulfill the goals of the Sinai Covenant they are still sanctified by the Ancestral Covenant. We share a common destiny - hence the reference to the Ancestral Covenant as Berit Goral - even if we do not share a common sense of purpose - the Sinai Covenant or Berit Yiud. Those inspired by the Ancestral Covenant appreciate whatever factor motivates Jews to identity with Judaism in whatever manner. It is no mystery why Rabbi Soloveitchik was a supporter of communication among all Jews. It was not a 'liberal' position per se. It follows from a strict reading of the demands of the Ancestral Covenant. Meeting with other Jews, marching with them in solidarity for Israel, participating in the Israeli government to enhance the welfare of the society are obligations - *hovah*, not *reshut*. These activities are required by the norms of no less a value than Ahavat Yisrael.

Covenant is a political concept. It tells us of a polis to which we belong, having entered it centuries ago. But, asks the modern Jew, what authority does that covenant have over us today. Why should we be concened about it, care for its norms, abide by its rules and statutes? Certainly, the question of the authority of tradition has been dominant in the modern period. This touches somewhat on both of the themes I am addressing - the challenge to the Jewish people and the challenge to Judaism. Here we see the modernity of the political notion of covenant. As rooted as it is in Biblical imagery it is also reminiscent of the writings of modern democratic political theorists who speak of a social contract which every citizen is part of no matter when the contract itself was initiated. So that my obligation to adhere to the laws of Canada, the United States, New York State or New York City derives from decisions, accords and commitments made centuries ago without my voice or agreement. Living today I inherit those obligations and the social covenant is renewed. If I am unhappy with any part of the system I can leave or try to change it. Living in the society automatically brings about covenantal responsibility. It is my consent to be part of the covenant. The authority of the social contract remains.

This political dimension is a strength of Rabbi Soloveitchik's approach. The Jewish polis, Am Yisrael, has a claim upon you and me as the sons and daughters of the covenant community which our ancestors founded.

It is my view that Rabbi Soloveitchik has here made an invaluable contribution to modern Jewish thought. The reality of the Jewish nation is firmly anchored in theological concepts. Jewish religion is not a product of Jewish national existence and experience; it is co-eval with it. The primacy of both Torah and nation are preserved. *Am Yisrael hai.*

NOTES

1. Quoted in *The Jew in The Modern World*, Paul R. Mendes-Flohr and Jehuda Reinharz, eds., p. 104. (Henceforth, JMW)

2. See the views of Abbe Gregoire, another supporter of Jewish emancipation. JMW, p.44. Shmuel Trigano offers an extensive analysis of the process in France in *The French Revolution and the Jews.* MODERN JUDAISM, Vol. 10, Number 2. May 1990.

3. See THE RAV SPEAKS: Five Addresses, Rabbi Joseph B. Soloveitchik. Tal Orot Institute, Jerusalem, 5743. Lecture 4, p. 127. My citations will be from here. He also discusses these issues in "Kol Dodi Dofek," a famous essay often reprinted. See the collection of essays edited by Pinchas Peli, IN ALONENESS, IN TOGETHERNESS, Orot, Jerusalem 5736, p. 331. (Hebrew) An English translation has been published by Lawrence Kaplan in THEOLOGICAL AND HALAKHIC REFLECTIONS ON THE HOLOCAUST, Bernhard H. Rosenberg and Fred Heuman, eds., Rabbinical Council of America, 1992.

THE SEPTUAGINT: THE FIRST TRANSLATION OF THE TORAH AND ITS EFFECTS

by Louis H. Feldman

Surely one of the greatest reformers in Jewish history was a non-Jew, Alexander the Great, who, in his brief lifetime in the fourth century B.C.E., did much to spread the Greek language and Greek thought among the various peoples that he conquered. From a Jewish point of view, the most important thing that he did was to establish cities, the most important being Alexandria in Egypt, where he invited Jews to settle and where, according to at least one papyrus fragment (Papyri Giessen University 5.46) dating from the first century C.E. the Jews numbered 180,000 in a total population of perhaps 500,000 to 600,00 - 30 to 36 percent of the whole.[1] Moreover, the Jews were either citizens or were granted isopolity (equal rights) with the Greeks (Josephus, *Against Apion* 2.38). Indeed, Josephus *Antiquities* 14.188) says explicitly that Julius Caesar in the first century B.C.E. set up a bronze tablet for the Jews in Alexandria declaring that they were citizens. Inasmuch as Alexandria within a century after its founding apparently displaced Athens as the cultural center of the Mediterranean world, the Jews, who until the fourth century B.C.E. had been largely farmers in Eretz Israel and

Babylonia, rather suddenly found themselves in large numbers in the midst of the leading center of Greek culture. In effect, Alexandria was the New York City of its day.

Our earliest papyri pertaining to the Jews of Egypt are in Aramaic, presumably reflecting the language that they brought with them from Eretz Israel; but within two generations, certainly by 270 B.C.E., the papyri are no longer in Aramaic but rather in Greek. It was approximately in that year, according to a number of sources—the Pseudepigraphic *Letter of Aristeas*; Philo, *Life of Moses* 2.5.25-7.44; Josephus, *Antiquities* 12.12-118; Talmud, *Megillah* 9a-b; *Soferim* 1.7—that Ptolemy II Philadelphia is said to have commissioned a translation on the island of Pharos off the coast of Alexandria by seventy or seventy-two (hence Septuagint) Jewish elders from Jerusalem of the Torah into Greek for the huge library which he was establishing in Alexandria. Whether his purpose in doing this was to show favor to the Jews, whose backing he needed inasmuch as he and his Macedonian and Greek followers amounted to no more than perhaps ten percent of the population of Egypt and hence he needed the support of the Jews as middlemen in administration and as soldiers in his army, there is certainly significance in the fact (*Letter of Aristeas 308*) that the translation, when completed, was presented first to the Jewish community and only thereafter (*Letter of Aristeas 312*) to King Ptolemy. Whether the translation was needed by the Jews to combat anti-Semitism, such as that embedded in the work by Manetho of about the same year, or to combat the Samaritan claims to the priority of their Torah, or perhaps to win converts to Judaism, certainly the translation was particularly useful since apparently the great majority of the Jews in Egypt by that time had forgotten their Hebrew and Aramaic.

In order to appreciate the effect of this translation we must realize that even if we are reading a document in the original there is a vast gap between the thought behind the language and the language itself. Just as no two people will play the score of a musical composition in exactly the same way, so also when we are translating a text, especially one which has so many different levels of meaning-and even containing a musical score (*trop*) as well. The Italians have a phrase: "*traduttore traditore*"-"a translator is a traitor." The translator is always in a dilemma. If the translation is literal, one is avoiding the issue of translation. Rabbi Judah bar Ilai (*Kiddushin* 49a) says that he who translates a verse literally is a liar and he who adds thereto is a blasphemer.

In our own day we may somewhat mitigate the problem by presenting alternative translations in parentheses or we may explain the translation in a footnote. In any case, we may place the original on a page facing the translation so that one may compare the two. In antiquity this was not done; and if a person did not know the original word in a text his only contact with the text was with the word used by the translator. What is particularly important about the Septuagint is that according to Philo (*Life of Moses* 2.7.37), who, himself being an Alexandrian, certainly knew the traditions about the translation, the translators "because, as it were possessed, and, under inspiration, wrote, not each several scribe something different, but the same word for word, as though dictated to each by an invisible prompter." Philo (*Life of Moses* 2.7.39) compares the translation to a work of geometry, in which the sense does not admit of variety of expression. He even goes to the extent of speaking of the translators as prophets and priests of the mysteries, "whose sincerity and singleness of thought has enabled them to go hand in hand with the purest of spirits, the spirit of Moses" (Life of Moses 2.7.40). Indeed, the Talmud (*Megillah* 9a) presents the translators as divinely inspired. As a result, although Ptolemy placed the elders in separate rooms, God prompted each of them so that independently they emerged with the same translation, even making certain deliberate changes, some of which are noted there, in order to avoid ambiguities or contradictions or theological problems or seeming insults to the royal family. It is not surprising, in view of such a remarkable tradition, that the leaders of the Jewish community (*Letter of Aristeas* 310-311) declared that since the translation was "in every respect accurate, it is right that it should remain in its present form and that no revision of any sort take place." When this was unanimously agreed to, a curse was pronounced upon any one who should add to or subtract from or modify the translation. Apparently, the Alexandrian Jews looked upon the translation as one is required to look upon the commandments in the Torah (Deuteronomy 4:2; cf. 12:32): "You shall not add to the word which I command you, nor take from it." Indeed, there is very good reason to believe that Philo, though writing treatise after treatise on the Torah, had little or no knowledge of the Hebrew original.[2] In fact, so far as we can tell, the Torah was read in the synagogue in Greek, if we may judge from the Cairo scroll of the Septuagint of Deuteronomy (Papyrus Fouad 266), dating from the first century B.C.E., which indicates that the reading was according to a triennial cycle.

Who were these translators, and what was their attitude toward their Jewish heritage and toward the Greek language and culture? According to the *Letter of Aristeas* (121), they were men of excellent education, thanks to their distinguished parentage, chosen by the high priest himself; and they had not only mastered Jewish literature but had also given considerable attention to the literature of the Greeks.[3] According to the *Letter of Aristeas* (235,296), at the banquet honoring the translators not only the king, but especially the philosophers who were present, expressed admiration for the translators. Indeed, the king is represented (*Letter of Aristeas* (321) as accounting it a privilege to be associated with such "cultured" men.

To be sure, the translators did, in some instances, make an effort to use distinctive vocabulary in referring to the Jewish religion as against paganism. In fact, whereas Scripture uses the same term, *mizbeah*, for both a Jewish and pagan altar, the Septuagint uses the Greek word *bomos* with reference to heathen worship, whereas it uses the word *thusiasterion*, a rare term in Greek cults, in referring to the altar of God. Additionally, the Septuagint distinguishes between a resident alien, *ger toshab*, whom they refer to by the common Hellenistic term of *paroikos*, and a stranger (*ger*) in Israel, whom they refer to by a term which they invent, *proselytos*. Significantly, also, the Septuagint uses the word *mantis* in referring to heathen soothsayers, whereas it reserves the word *prophetes* when speaking of Hebrew prophets. Again, whereas the usual Greek word for a votive offering is *anathema*, the Septuagint translated the Hebrew *Korban* as *doron*. Likewise, whereas in pagan religious terminology *euphemia* is used to indicate words of good omen, prayer, and praise, the Septuagint uses the word *eulogia*, which in Greek usually means simply "praise" and does not belong to cultic language, to translate the religious term *berakhah*. Furthermore, the Greek word *alsos*, which in pagan terminology means "sacred precinct," is used in the Septuagint only with reference to the pagan *asherah*, some kind of cult object made out of wood. Moreover, when speaking of images of pagan deities the translators never use the common Greek terms *agalma* or *eikon* but rather use *eidolon* (our English word "idol"), which really means "phantom." Finally, one would have expected the translators to use the word *monos*, "alone," frequently in referring to a monotheistic religion; yet, it is found only once (Deuteronomy 32:12). Presumably, the reason why this word is avoided is that it commonly occurs in Greek prayers referring to the superiority of the god in question to other deities. Likewise, although one would have expected the translators to use the word *protos*, "first," in referring to God, they never use it, most likely because the pagan Greeks use it often in their hymns in referring to their gods; rather, they prefer *heis*, "one."

Nevertheless, the translators did introduce foreign concepts in their translation of certain major terms. In particular, they usually render the word "Torah" by *nomos*. The literate Greek, reading this word and not aware that it stands for Torah, would think of the passage in Herodotus (3.38), the popular father of history, in which the Persian king Darius asked the Greeks what price would persuade them to eat their fathers' dead bodies (the custom of the Indians) and asked the Indians what price would persuade them to burn their fathers' dead bodies (the custom of the Greeks). Each was horrified, whereupon Herodotus quotes Pindar, "Custom [*nomos*] is king." Again, the most popular Greek playwright, Sophocles, presents in his *Antigone* a contrast between *nomos*, man-made law as espoused by Creon, and *physis*, natural law as espoused by Antigone. But Torah is not custom and is not man-made. It is "instruction" or "direction" in the broadest sense. It includes both *halakhah* (law) and *haggadah* (lore). The Torah includes much more than commandments; significantly, it includes history as well. Indeed, when the Psalmist (78.1) says "Give ear, O my people, to my Torah," what follows is a history of the Jewish people focusing on the Exodus and the entrance into Eretz Israel. We may sense the influence of this Septuagintal view of the Torah as law in the antinomianism implicit in Philo's preference for allegorical interpretation of the Torah; for, he says (*On Joseph* 6.28), "broadly speaking, all or most of the law-book is an allegory." Nevertheless, to be sure, he is critical of those (*On the Migration of Abraham* 16.89) who are overpunctilious about seeing symbolism in the laws while they treat the literal sense of the laws with easygoing neglect. It is clear that he has these excessive allegorists in mind when he excoriates (*On the Migration of Abraham* 16.91) those who violate the rules of the Sabbath by lighting fires, tilling the ground, carrying loads, instituting proceedings in court, acting as jurors, and demanding the restoration of deposits or recovering loans. It is not surprising that Paul can speak of the abrogation of the *Nomos*, thus giving it a narrow and pejorative connotation as a legalistic religion. A law can be repealed; the Torah is eternal. Sometimes, as Franz Rosenzweig put it, history is made in a dictionary.

Again, in rendering the word *emunah* by *pistis*, the Septuagint is using a word which in Plato's *Republic* (7.533E-534A), the most influential of philosophical works during the Hellenistic Age, refers to a mere opinion about real things and is, in fact, the next to the lowest degree of human knowledge. Moreover, as Martin Buber points out in his *Two Types of Faith*, *pistis* is faith that something is, that is, an intellectual belief, whereas *emunah* is faith and unconditional trust in. Indeed, for the Greeks to believe in the gods is for them to be convinced intellectually that they exist.

For the word *hesed*, which combines the concepts of pity and piety, the Greek really has no equivalent. The Septuagint usually renders this by the word *eleemosyne*, "pity." But this word generally has negative connotations, as we see notably in Aristotle's *Poetics* (13.1452B30-32), where it is an undesirable emotion which is purged out of one's system by watching tragic drama. For Spinoza pity is *muliebris misericordia*, "womanish pity," clearly disparaging to both women and pity. On the other hand, mercy (*rahamim*, Exodus 34:6) is one of the attributes of God. Indeed, the Tetragrammaton itself connotes mercy. According to the prophet Micah (6:8) one of the three qualities which God requires of humans is to love mercy. The Hebrew word *rahamim* is said to be derived from the word *rehem*, "womb," as if to say that the womb generates pity. In contrast, the Greek word for "womb," *hystera*, generates not pity but hysteria. To render the word *hasid*, as the Septuagint usually does, by the Greek word *hosios*, "religious," "devout," "holy," loses the connotation of kindness and mercy and reduces religion to performing religious duties as such.

In Hebrew the word *nefesh* has a wide range of meaning: soul, life, vital spirit, mind, self, person, living creature, anyone. It may even refer to a dead being. The Septuagint consistently translates the word by the Greek *psyche*, which, to be sure, also has a wide range of meaning: breath, life, spirit, ghost, soul, mind, reason, understanding. However, we must try to put ourselves in the mindset of readers in the Hellenistic period. Inasmuch as Socrates and Plato were the most popular and most influential of Greek philosophers during this period,[4] when seeing the word *psyche* the reader would think of its contrast with the word *soma*, "body," especially as discussed in Plato's *Phaedo*. According to Plato, the body is the prisonhouse of the soul, and death is to be welcomed as an opportunity for the soul to flit free from that confinement. In Jewish thought, however, the body and the soul form a harmonious unity; at the resurrection God will judge body and soul as one. When Philo (*On the Migration of Abraham* 6.26) uses the image of athletic combat to express the fight of the soul against the body and its passions, he is reflecting the Platonic view implicit in the Septuagint's translation.

Again, in rendering the word *zedek* by the Greek word *dikaiosyne* the translators were introducing a concept that relates, on the one hand, to social customs and institutions, as seen in the popular definition of *dikaiosyne* as "rendering every man his due" (Plato, *Republic* (1.331 E3-4) and, on the other hand, to an abstract epistemological principle, as Plato defines it in the Republic as a Form or Idea which is the harmony of wisdom, courage, and temperance. For the Greeks it is an abstract intellectual idea; for the Jews it is righteousness, the humanitarian virtue par excellence, benevolence that goes beyond one's legal obligations.

The translation of *berith* in the Septuagint by *diatheke* is similarly misleading. The Hebrew word, at least initially, does not mean "agreement" or "covenant" or "alliance." Rather, it refers to the relationship of a master to his subject, through which he protects the latter unilaterally. The Greek word originally meant "promise" or "pledge." It later came to mean "disposition of property by will" or "testament"; and, indeed, in the Talmud (e.g. *Baba Mezia* 152b) *di'athiki* refers to a disposition of property, especially by will and testament.

Moreover, in rendering the Hebrew Tetragrammaton by the Greek word *Kyrios* ("L-rd") the translators were employing a word which is common in the mystery religions, so popular among the Greeks. Again, in translating 'Elyon ("Highest") with reference to God by the Greek word *hypsistos,* "highest," they were applying to God the epithet which was applied particularly to Zeus (Pindar, *Nemean Odes* 1.60 etc.). Moreover, the term is used of the deity Sabazios.[5] And yet, we have even found an inscription (*Corpus Inscriptionum Judaicarum* 2.1443), dating from the second or first century B.C.E., recording that a synagogue in Egypt was dedicated to God the Most High (*hypsistos*). Indeed, in the *Letter of Aristeas* (15-16), the alleged author, Aristeas, who is represented as a non-Jew but whom scholars generally regard as actually a Jew, is quoted as telling King Ptolemy Philadelphus that "the same God who has given them their law guides your kingdom also, as I have learned in my researches. God, the overseer and creator of all things, whom they worship, is He whom all men worship; and we too, Your Majesty, though we address Him differently, as Zeus and Dis; by these names men of old not suitably signified that He through whom all creatures receive life and come into being is the guide and lord of all." Hence Zeus and God are equated as a single divine principle. In fact, the Septuagint goes further in rendering *Elohim lo tekallel* (Exodus 22:27) as *theous ou kakologeseis,* "You shall not curse gods," whereas the rabbinic tradition (*Sanhedrin 66a*) understands this to mean "You shall not curse judges." Indeed, and very significantly, both Philo (*De Specialibus Legibus* 1.9.53) and Josephus (*Antiquities* 4.207, *Against Apion* 2.237), who adopt the Septuagint's translation here, explain that the reason for this injunction is that the very word "God" is sacred. In contrast to this liberalism, we may note that the Torah itself (Deuteronomy 7.25) requires that Israelites burn the graven images of the Canaanites.

In particular, we may note the importance of the Septuagint's translation of the admittedly obscure name of God as *eh'yeh asher eh'yeh* ("I am that I am," Exodus 3:14) by *ego eimi ho on* ("I am the One who is"). In Philo (*De Somniis* 1.39.230) this becomes *to on*, "that which is," thus converting the personal God of Judaism into the Platonic Absolute of philosophy.[6]

We may surmise that the Greek reader of the Septuagint would perceive Platonic influence in the translation of *tohu vabohu* (Genesis 1:2, "without form and void") as *aoratos kai akataskeuastos* ("unseen and unformed"), the implication being that prior to the creation of the visible world was the creation of the invisible world, a key Platonic doctrine. Indeed, Philo (*On the Account of the World's Creation Given by Moses* 7.29, 10.36-37) thus explains the so-called two accounts of creation in the opening chapters of Genesis.

The heart of Platonism is the method of dialectic. The key statement of Socrates is (Plato, *Apology* 38A5) *ho anexetastos bios ou biotos anthropoi*, "the unexamined life is not worth living for a human being." This examination (or cross-examination or criticism), which Plato elsewhere (e.g., *Phaedrus* 276A) refers to as *elegkhos*, requires a readiness to question all facile assumptions. It is, therefore, particularly significant that the Septuagint translates *hokheah tokhiah eth 'amithekha* (Leviticus 19:17, "You shall surely rebuke your neighbor") as *elegkhoi elegxeis ton plesion sou* ("You shall cross-examine your neighbor with cross-examination").

Perhaps the most important consequence of the elevation of the Septuagint is that it was regarded by the most influential Jewish thinkers of Alexandria, Aristobulus (second century B.C.E.) and Philo (ca. 20 B.C.E.-40 C.E.) as being consonant with Plato. The former (cited by Eusebius, *Praeparatio Evangelica* 13.12.1) asserts that "It is clear that Plato followed the tradition of the law that we use, and he is conspicuous for having worked through each of the details contained in it." Realizing that the question might arise as to how Plato could have known the Torah before the Septuagint, he presents the thesis (*ibid.*) that there had been translations even before the Septuagint and, in fact, even before the Persian conquest (525 B.C.E.).[7] As for Philo, who declares (*On the Change of Names* 39.223) that he philosophizes "according to Moses," he describes Plato as "most sacred" (*Every Good Man Is Free* 2.13) and he never openly disagrees with him. Indeed, it became proverbial that "either Plato philonizes or Philo platonizes" (Jerome, *Concerning Illustrious Men* 11). Plato's alleged indebtedness to the Greek Bible likewise became proverbial (e.g., Numenius of Apamea cited by Clement of Alexandria, *Stromata* 1.22.150.4): "What is Plato but Moses speaking in Attic Greek?" In fact, Philo's popularity with the early Christian Church is due in part, at least, to the fact that he was regarded as the interpreter *par excellence* of the allegorical interpretation of the Septuagint version.[8] We may sense the influence of the Septuagint as reconciled with Plato upon Philo's nephew, Tiberius Julius Alexander, who, as a young man, appears in one of Philo's philosophical treatises, *On Providence* (fragments 1 and 2), and asks why, if God created the world, just four elements were taken and how one can maintain the existence of Providence when there is so much injustice in the world. Apparently, the uncle's answers proved unsatisfactory, inasmuch as we find that the nephew, who eventually reached the high offices of procurator of Judaea (Josephus, *Antiquities* 20.100-103), governor of the most important province of the Roman Empire, Egypt (Josephus, *Jewish War* 2.309), and second in command to Titus at the Roman siege of Jerusalem (*Jewish War* 5.45-46, 510; 6.237-242), "did not remain faithful to his ancestral customs," as Josephus (*Antiquities* 20.100) puts it.

Ancient Alexandria apparently had many synagogues (Philo, *Embassy to Gaius* 20.132), including one which was so large and so beautiful that the Talmud (*Sukkah* 51b) quotes Rabbi Judah as saying that one who has not seen it has never seen the glory of Israel. But Alexandria apparently had no yeshivot. Nevertheless, intermarriage was not a major problem; when Philo (*On the Special Laws* 3.5.29) does mention it, he speaks of its consequences not in his own day but at some vague time in the future. Presumably the sheer number of Jews and their concentration in certain areas, together with the virulent anti-Semitism which pervaded Egypt at this time, made such unions less likely.[9] Apostasy was also apparently infrequent.[10] Rather, the more common method of expressing deviation from the Jewish tradition was probably simply non-observance. We may find a clue in Philo's comment (*On the Special Laws* 1.35.186) that the fast of the Day of Atonement is carefully observed not only by those who are zealous for piety but also by those who never act religiously in the rest of their life.

The Rabbis themselves apparently had second thoughts about the Septuagint translation, especially after it became the official version of the Christian Church, so that a Church Father such as Justin Martyr (*Dialogue with Trypho*) regarded it as more authentic than even the Hebrew original. Whereas in *Megillah* 9a the Rabbis speak of the translators as being divinely inspired, in *Soferim* (1:7) they compare the day when the translation was completed to the day when the Golden Calf was built. No one can doubt the beauty of the Greek language and of much of Greek literature. Indeed, this is acknowledged in Noah's blessing in the Torah itself (Genesis 9:27): "May God enlarge Japheth" (the ancestor of the Greeks), a passage quoted by the Talmud (*Megillah* 9b) shortly after relating the story of the translation. But the blessing is "may he [Japheth] dwell in the tents of Shem," rather than the reverse. The main question is: which is primary, the Hebrew or the Greek Philo read Plato in the original but the Torah in Greek. Maimonides read Aristotle in translation but the Torah in the original.

NOTES

1. See Diana Delia, "The Population of Roman Alexandria," *Trasactions of the American Philological Association* 118 (1988) 286-288.

2. See my *Jew and Gentile in the Ancient World: Attitudes and Interactions from Alexander to Justinian* (Princeton: Princeton University Press, 1993) 55. If Philo had known the Hebrew original one would have expected him to cite it, especially where it differed from the Septuagint. Moreover, despite his voluminous writings, he never cites the name of even a single rabbi of the time.

3. Similarly, Philo (*Life of Moses* 2.6.32) asserts that the high priest, in

selecting the translators, sought those "who had received an education in Greek as well as in their native lore."

4. See Moses Hadas, "Plato in Hellenistic Fusion" *Journal of the History of Ideas* 19 (1958) 3-13.

5. See my *Jew and Gentile in the Ancient World*, 74.

6. See Morton Smith, "The Image of God," *Bulletin of the John Rylands Library* 40 (1958) 474.

7. A papyrus from Oxyrhynchus (41.2944) suggests that at least some biblical themes were known to the Greeks even before the death of Plato. See Joseph Mélèze Modrzejewski, *The Jews of Egypt from Rameses II to Emperor Hadrian* (Philadelphia: Jewish Publication Society, 1995) 66. However, we have not a single fragment of any translation before the Septuagint.

8. See David T. Runia, *Philo in Early Christian Literature: A Survey* (Assen: Van Gorcum, 1993).

9. Among the by now many thousands of papyri that we have there is only one unambiguous mention, dating from the second century B.C.E., of an intermarriage between a Jew and a non-Jew (Berlin Papyrus no. 11641 [unpublished]).

10. See my *Jew and Gentile in the Ancient World*, 79-83; and Modrzejewski, *The Jews of Egypt*, 56-61.

WHY DIDN'T HE DO IT?

AN ANALYSIS OF WHY DAVID DID NOT KILL SAUL

by Hayyim Angel

I   INTRODUCTION

When Saul was afflicted with his *ru'ah ra'ah* (a psychological disorder), he hurls spears at David, attempts to set his children Jonathan and Michal against him, and personally pursues David with the royal army. He does all this although David had killed Goliath, had served as Saul's arms-bearer and musician, and had been an extremely devoted soldier.

Even more astonishing than Saul's violent behavior towards David, however, is David's persistent love and compassion for Saul. The first time David has the chance to kill Saul, David's men view the opportunity as a divine blessing. David, however, emphatically rejects his men's request:

> David's men said to him, "This is the day of which the Lord said to you, 'I will deliver your enemy into your hands; you can do with him as you please.'" David went and stealthily cut off the corner of Saul's cloak. But afterward David reproached himself for cutting off the corner of Saul's cloak. He said to

> his men, "The Lord forbid that I should do such a thing to my
> lord-the Lord's anointed-that I should raise my hand against
> him; for he is the Lord's anointed." David rebuked his men
> and did not permit them to attack Saul (I Sam. 24:5-8).[1]

Not only does David not kill Saul himself, but he stops his
men from doing so. David settles for cutting off the corner of
Saul's coat, and later regrets even having done this trivial act
against God's anointed.

Two chapters later, David again has an opportunity to
eliminate Saul. Abishai (one of David's loyal supporters, who
becomes a military leader once David is king) wants to deliver
the fatal blow to Saul; but again, David strongly opposes such
an action:

> And Abishai said to David, "God has delivered your enemy
> into your hands today. Let me pin him to the ground with a
> single thrust of the spear. I will not have to strike him twice."
> But David said to Abishai, "Don't do him violence! No one
> can lay hands on the Lord's anointed with impunity" (I Sam.
> 26:8-9).

David expresses his allegiance to Saul most poignantly
after the latter perishes in battle. The eulogy, found in II Sam.
1:17-27, ostensibly reveals that David's kindness towards Saul
was not feigned; David really loved Saul. "Your glory, O Israel,
lies slain on your heights; How the mighty have fallen" (II
Sam. 1:19). David orders the execution of the youth who
claimed to have sealed Saul's doom (II Sam. 1:13-16).

Even with our awareness of David's greatness and piety, it
is difficult to imagine that he could have harbored no
resentment towards Saul. Ralbag and Abarbanel (I Sam. 24:5)
suggest that in addition to the more religious motivations
stopping David from killing Saul, David indeed did have an

ulterior motive for not killing the king: David knew that he was to succeed Saul as King of Israel. David reasoned that if he were to assassinate the first king, perhaps someone else might decide to assassinate the second king, i.e., David himself. Ralbag and Abarbanel (II Sam. 1:14) go on to assert that it was for the same reason that David ordered the youth executed-David wanted to make it clear that regicide is an unforgivable crime.[2] While affirming that David was partially motivated by piety, Ralbag and Abarbanel assert that his actions also included a more practical impetus for his exceptional restraint.

One's attitude towards David (not to mention one's approach when studying biblical heroes in general) undoubtedly will affect whether one inclines towards the purer portrayal of David, or whether one incorporates the more utilitarian dimension suggested by Ralbag and Abarbanel. But perhaps we have a more objective method of weighing the two positions, using a source which we have for no other biblical character: the Psalms.

It is unusual for a biblical narrative to supply the feelings or motivations for the actions of a given character. Instead, the Bible generally focuses on actions, and permits the reader to speculate about the deeper aspects of a character's soul. However, we have at least a partial record of what David was feeling while being pursued by Saul, and how he reacted when the king was killed in battle. By analyzing David's personal reflections and feelings in the Psalms, we may attain a more comprehensive picture of the relationship between David and Saul. In this essay, we will consider the Psalms which David composed while fleeing Saul, and show how these Psalms can influence our understanding of the narratives in the Book of Samuel.

II METHODOLOGICAL CONSIDERATIONS

There are seven Psalms where the superscription indicates a specific event during Saul's pursuit of David.[3]

1. Psalm 18: For the leader. Of David, the servant of the Lord, who addressed the words of this song to the Lord after the Lord had saved him from the hands of all his enemies, and from the clutches of Saul (see I Sam. 31:6).

2. Psalm 52: For the leader. A *maskil* of David, when Doeg the Edomite came and informed Saul, telling him, "David came to Ahimelech's house" (see I Sam. 22:9-10).

3. Psalm 54: For the leader; with instrumental music. A *maskil* of David, when the Ziphites came and told Saul, "Know, David is hiding among us" (see I Sam. 23:14; 26:1).

4. Psalm 57: For the leader; *al tashhet.* Of David. A *michtam*; when he fled from Saul into a cave (see I Sam. 22:1; 24:3).

5. Psalm 59: For the leader; *al tashhet.* Of David. A *michtam*; when Saul sent men to watch his house in order to put him to death (see I Sam. 19:11-17).

6. Psalm 63: A psalm of David, when he was in the Wilderness of Judah (see I Sam. 23:14; 23:24; 24:1; 25:1).

7. Psalm 142: A *maskil* of David, while he was in the cave. A prayer (see I Sam. 22:1; 24:3).[4]

Although one might assume that all prayers expressed in these seven Psalms reflect David's feelings towards Saul and his men (with the exception of Psalm 52, which discusses Doeg, and 54, which criticizes the Ziphites), the matter is not so simple. There are two methodological questions which we must address:

1. In these Psalms, was David praying exclusively for himself (and the Psalm later became canonized for others to use), or did David originally consider his prayers as a formula for others to use for many related occasions, regardless of what David was experiencing as he wrote them?

2. How close is the relationship between the body of a Psalm with its superscription? Must we assume that the entire Psalm reflects the event specified in the superscription, or is it possible that the Psalm extrapolates to broader circumstances, beyond the original event which inspired its composition?

A. What was the original purpose of the Psalms?

The Talmud (Pesahim 117a) leaves the first issue unresolved:

> Our rabbis have taught: all the songs and hymns which David said in the book of Psalms, R. Eliezer says, he wrote them for himself. R. Joshua says, he wrote them for the community. The Sages say, some are for the community, and others are for himself: those in the singular voice are for himself, while those in the plural voice are for the community.

According to R. Eliezer, David wrote all his Psalms as private prayers for himself. Later, these Psalms were publicized and canonized, making them accessible to others. R. Joshua asserts the opposite position: David originally intended the Psalms to be communal prayers, and therefore formulated them in more general terms so that they could be used for a wide array of occasions. The Sages adopt a middle position: those Psalms in the first person singular were originally private prayers of David. Those Psalms in a plural voice were written originally as communal prayers.

The five Psalms which we will consider (18, 57, 59, 63 and 142) all are written in the first person singular. According to both R. Eliezer and the Sages, then, these five Psalms were composed originally as private prayers, in which David pleaded to God to save him from Saul and his men. However, according to R. Joshua, even these five Psalms were written as communal prayers, addressing crises beyond David's personal life.

The contrast between the two positions is striking: if David composed these Psalms as private prayers, then one may assume that references to "enemies" allude specifically to Saul and his men. If, however, the Psalms were formulated as prayers for the entire community, then David may have included more generic elements, including details not directly relevant to Saul's pursuit of David. Alternatively, one could argue that our version of the Psalms has been subsequently reworked, leaving out David's personal feelings and references.

B. What is the relationship between the superscription and the body of the Psalm?

Closely related to the issue of the original intent of a Psalm is whether the entire body of a Psalm must correspond to the introductory verse, or superscription. For example, Psalm 59 begins, For the leader; *al tashhet*. Of David. A *michtam*; when Saul sent men to watch his house in order to put him to death. This superscription alludes to the narrative in I Sam. 19:11-17, where Michal helps her husband David escape Saul's men. The beginning of this Psalm reads:

2. Save me from my enemies, O my God; secure me against my assailants.

3. Save me from evildoers, deliver me from murderers.

4. For see, they lie in wait for me; fierce men plot against me for no offense of mine, for no transgression, O Lord;

5. For no guilt of mine do they rush to array themselves against me. Look, rouse Yourself on my behalf!

6. You, O Lord God of hosts, God of Israel, bestir Yourself to bring all nations to account; have no mercy on any treacherous villain (Psa. 59:2-6).

In general, Psalms do not make references to specific events (with the exception of the superscriptions).[5] Were one to assume a direct relationship between a Psalm's specific superscription and its main body, then in this case, all general references to "enemies" would be to Saul and his men. If, on the other hand, the main body of the Psalm may exceed the boundaries of its superscription, then one would not necessarily be able to associate every reference to David's feelings towards Saul and his men (but instead would conclude that this Psalm was composed as a general prayer, asking God to save oppressed people from their enemies).

This issue comes to the fore in verse six, "You, O Lord God of hosts, God of Israel, bestir Yourself to bring *all nations* to account; have no mercy on any treacherous villain." In this verse (and in verse 9 also), David apparently refers to other nations. This allusion seems to support those who contend that the body of a Psalm may refer to events beyond those mentioned in the superscription. Amos Hakham (*Da'at Mikra*), adopts the position of R. Joshua (that all Psalms were composed for the public, rather than specifically relating to David's personal experiences), that this verse in fact is a general prayer, applicable to all enemies of David and the Israelite nation.

Yet, most traditional exegetes state that even these ostensibly explicit references to other nations still refer to Saul and his men, following the superscription:

> Rashi (v. 6): "Bestir Yourself to bring all nations to account"-may You judge the wicked people *as You would the nations*. On them You should have no mercy (cf. his comments to v. 9, and Metzudat David).

> Radak (v. 9): As You mock all the nations who deny You-annulling their [evil] thoughts and plots, so too may You mock these [i.e., Saul and his men]..[6]

> Ibn Ezra (v. 6): "Do not have mercy on traitors"-from whichever nation they derive (i.e., even if they are from Israel).

It would appear that in this case, Rashi, Radak, and Ibn Ezra all follow the view that 1) David originally composed this Psalm as a personal prayer for salvation from Saul and his men; and 2) *All* references to enemies in this Psalm allude to Saul and his men (even those where the plain sense of the text would have indicated otherwise).

Malbim takes a middle position in his explication of this verse. He interprets the first half of the verse, "bestir Yourself to bring *all nations* to account," as a reference to the other nations. According to Malbim, David is concerned that while he flees Saul, nobody is protecting Israel from its outside enemies; therefore, David implores God to protect Israel. Malbim then explicates the second half of the verse, "have no mercy on any treacherous villain," as a reference to Saul and his men. Thus, Malbim maintains that the entire Psalm follows its superscription, while keeping the simple sense of the text intact.

Clearly, the methodological issues involved in an analysis of Psalms, even those with specific historical superscriptions, are complex and difficult to resolve. As we consider the five Psalms which David composed and addressed towards Saul and his men, we will begin with the assumption that David composed these Psalms as private prayers, and that the main bodies of the Psalms follow their superscriptions. At the end of our analysis of the Psalms, we will address the opposing position regarding our inquiry.

III THE PSALMS

A. Psalm 142

1. A *maskil* of David, while he was in the cave. A prayer...

5. Look at my right and see-I have no friend, there is nowhere I can flee, no one cares about me...

7. Listen to my cry, for I have been brought very low; save me from my pursuers, for they are too strong for me.

8. Free me from my prison, that I may praise Your Name. The righteous shall glory in me for Your gracious dealings with me.

Psalm 142 appears consistent with the image of purity portrayed in the narratives in Samuel. While hiding in a cave from Saul and his men (either in I Sam. 22:1, or 24:3), David feels isolated and frightened. Despite the great threat to his life, however, he does not ask that God obliterate his enemies, nor does he even ridicule them; instead, he asks only that God deliver him from his adversaries.

Reading this Psalm, one feels the profound anguish which

plagued David as he fled from his beloved father-in-law, King Saul. Yet, one cannot underestimate David's religious resolve, as he asks to be spared so that God's Name will be sanctified among righteous people (v. 8).

B. Psalm 57

Yet, Psalm 142 stands alone in conveying this theme of David's purity. In Psalm 57, another prayer composed while David hid in a cave from Saul, David laments in a different, more hostile, tone:

1. For the leader; *al tashhet*. Of David. A *michtam*; when he fled from Saul into a cave.

2. Have mercy on me, O God, have mercy on me, for I seek refuge in You...

4. He will reach down from heaven and deliver me: God will send down His steadfast love; my persecutor reviles.

5. As for me, I lie down among man-eating lions whose teeth are spears and arrows, whose tongue is a sharp sword.

7. They prepared a net for my feet to ensnare me; they dug a pit for me, but they fell into it.

8. My heart is firm, O God; my heart is firm; I will sing, I will chant a hymn.

In this Psalm, David continues the themes from Psalm 142, praying for salvation, and remaining steadfastly focused on God and His reputation. But in this Psalm, David describes his pursuers in negative terms, poetically depicting their brutality and viciousness (vv. 4-5). Additionally, David appears gratified that his antagonists have fallen into the snare which they had set for David (v.7).[7]

C. Psalm 59

In Psalm 59, when Saul sends his men to surround David's house (see I Sam. 19), David appears even more resentful of Saul and his men:

3. Save me from evildoers, deliver me from murderers.

4. For see, they lie in wait for me; fierce men plot against me for no offense of mine, for no transgression, O Lord;

5. For no guilt of mine do they rush to array themselves against me. Look, rouse Yourself on my behalf!

7. They come each evening growling like dogs, roaming the city.

8. They rave with their mouths...9. But You, O Lord, laugh at them...

12. Do not kill them lest my people be unmindful; with Your power make wanderers of them; bring them low, O our Shield, the Lord.

13. ...Let them be trapped by their pride, and by the imprecations and lies they utter.

14. Your fury put an end to them; put an end to them that they be no more; that it may be known to the ends of the earth that God does rule over Jacob. Selah.

This Psalm contains the elements we have seen in the others: prayer for salvation from enemies (vv. 2-3, 10-11), and the request for the sanctification of God's Name (v. 14). However, David displays even more hostility towards Saul and his men, calling them dogs, the lowliest of all animals.[8] Even more astonishingly, David calls on God to destroy his enemies, but to do so slowly, so that all people can witness their demise, and realize that God is against them (see Rashi, Radak, and Metzudat David on 59:12). One begins to sense that David indeed harbored much resentment toward Saul and his men, both for threatening his life, and for pursuing him.

D. Psalm 63

Psalm 63 (written when David was in the Wilderness of Judah) prays even more directly for the demise of Saul and his men:

2. God, You are my God; I search for You, my soul thirsts for You, my body yearns for You, as a parched and thirsty land that has no water.

10. May those who seek to destroy my life enter the depths of the earth.

11. May they be gutted by the sword; may they be prey for jackals.[9]

12. But the king [i.e., David[10]] shall rejoice in God; all who swear by Him shall exult, when the mouth of liars is stopped.

There is no question, then, that David did harbor much anger towards Saul and his men, praying for their destruction, using harsh language against them, and even promising to praise God at their downfall.

E. Psalm 18

David was so excited by Saul's death,[11] that he composed Psalm 18 (found in variant form in II Sam. 22), a Psalm of triumph over his enemies. "To the chief musician, of David, the servant of the Lord, who spoke to the Lord the words of this song on the day that the Lord delivered him from the hand of all his enemies, and from the hand of Saul" (Psa. 18:1).[12] This Psalm is a fitting epilogue to the other Saul-related Psalms of David.[13]

In conclusion, David felt resentment toward Saul and his men throughout the pursuit. While maintaining allegiance to God and praying for his own personal salvation as well as the sanctification of God's Name, David also expresses deep bitterness towards his enemies.

This analysis is based on the assumption that these Psalms in fact were written originally with Saul and his men in mind, as indicated by the superscriptions. Even were one to follow the opinion of R. Joshua, that all Psalms were composed originally for the community, one still may argue that David drew his inspiration from the events that were occurring as he wrote the Psalms.

According to Amos Hakham, Psalms are always written in generic formulas, so that they are applicable to a plethora of different situations. One may not draw conclusions from possible allusions to Saul and his men, since they may refer to any enemies.

However, most traditional commentators maintain a more direct relationship between a superscription and the main body of the Psalm. In our analysis of 59:6 above, we saw that even where David refers to "the nations," many commentators still maintain that even this verse refers to Saul and his men. Certainly in almost all instances regarding general references to "enemies," our exegetes maintain that they refer to the subject of the superscription; in our case, to Saul and his men.[14]

Hence, one may conclude that within the opinions of most

traditional commentators, the five Psalms we have considered point directly to David's feelings towards Saul and his men during various stages of the pursuit.

IV THE TEXT OF SAMUEL

After reading and analyzing the Psalms, we may reconsider some of the passages in the book of Samuel pertaining to the relationship between David and Saul. In II Sam. 4, Ish Boshet (Saul's son who had succeeded his father with Abner's help) is murdered. As with the Amalekite youth in chapter one, David has the assassins put to death. Abarbanel again argues that David wanted to protect the institution of monarchy, specifically in his own self-interest. Hence the strict and immediate punishment meted out to the assassins of a different Israelite monarch.

More significant, however, is David's *a fortiori* reasoning which he employs in justification of his killing Ish Boshet's assassins:

> The man who told me in Ziklag that Saul was dead thought he was bringing good news. But instead of rewarding him for the news, I seized him and killed him. How much more, then, when wicked people have killed a blameless man in bed in his own house! I will certainly avenge his blood on you, and I will rid the earth of you (II Sam 4:10-11).

From this statement, we may infer that David believed that Saul was not righteous (i.e., he deserved his death), and that only Ish Boshet was unjustly killed. Although David's reasoning may be understood in several other ways, this explanation is consistent with David's Psalms. Perhaps David still harbored anger towards Saul.

We find further evidence of David's continued resentment towards Saul when Michal (Saul's daughter and David's wife) becomes enraged after seeing David dancing immodestly around the Ark. After Michal censures David for his unkingly mode of dress and behavior, David snaps back at her,

> It was before the Lord who chose me instead of your father and all his family and appointed me ruler over the Lord's people Israel! (II Sam. 6:21).

In the text itself, David seems rather quick to rub in Saul's loss of the kingdom to Michal. Midrashic insight on this discussion is even more striking:

> Said Michal, "My father's kingdom was more becoming than yours, for far be it from any of [his family] to be viewed with even a forearm or calf exposed..." Answered David, "...[The members of] your father's household sought but their own honor, forsaking the honor of Heaven. And I do not do so..." (*Midrash Samuel* 25:6).

Both text and Midrash capture David's rancor which he apparently nurtured against Saul even after the latter's demise.

When David searches for a relative of Saul to honor, he asks, "Is there anyone left of the House of Saul with whom I can keep faith *for the sake of Jonathan*" (II Sam. 9:1)? Not for Saul's sake! To be sure, Jonathan was a great friend of David; nevertheless, David does not here display love of Saul which he had seemingly shown when Saul had pursued him.

On a more speculative level, the eulogy which David gave for Saul and Jonathan also may reflect anger towards Saul. While mourning both for their military valor and heroism, only Jonathan gets special mention as one whom David loved: "I grieve for you, my brother Jonathan, you were most dear to me. Your love was wonderful to me more than the love of women" (II Sam. 1:26). Again, while it is obvious that David was closer with Jonathan than with Saul, it seems peculiar that David would completely omit any personal feelings for Saul; David praises Saul only for his military accomplishments. Alsheikh suggests that David recited this eulogy publicly, so that nobody would think that David was happy about Saul's death. Of course, we have seen that David was at least partially joyful at Saul's demise, composing Psalm 18 in his gratitude. Alsheikh's interpretation thus serves to support our speculation about David's eulogy of Saul.

Let us turn back to David's stunning restraint from killing Saul in both chapters:

> "As the Lord lives, the Lord Himself will strike him down, or his time will come and he will die; or he will go down to battle and perish. But the Lord forbid that I should lay a hand on the Lord's anointed" (26:10-11)!

Although David admirably stops himself and Abishai from assassinating Saul, he simultaneously prays for the death of the monarch through natural causes! These verses, read in light of the Psalms we have seen, capture the powerful emotional conflict David felt at those moments.

The text appears to portray David's mixed feelings towards Saul in chapter 24, his first opportunity to kill the monarch:

> "...Please, sir, take a close look at the corner of your cloak in my hand; for when I cut off the corner of your cloak, I did not kill you. You must see plainly that I have done nothing evil or rebellious, and I have never wronged you. Yet you are bent on taking my life.
>
> *May the Lord judge between you and me! And may he take*

vengeance upon you for me, but my hand will never touch you...

Against whom has the king of Israel come out? Whom are you pursuing? A dead dog? A single flea?

May the Lord be arbiter and may He judge between you and me! May He take note and uphold my cause, and vindicate me against you" (24:12-16)!

David, in his extended plea to Saul, appears to oscillate between a position of love and humility (please, sir...against whom has the king of Israel come out), and one of hostility and vengeance (may the Lord judge...)! From our above analysis of the Psalms, it seems that David is caught in between his profound love for his father-in-law and God's anointed, and his equally potent hostility towards his ruthless pursuer.

V CONCLUSIONS

From the Psalms which David composed while being pursued by Saul, we find that David's feelings towards Saul were far more complex than a casual reading of the later chapters in I Samuel would suggest. Additionally, we have seen that David did not forget Saul's conduct toward him too quickly; David's outburst at Michal, and more subtle references in the stories of Ish Boshet, Mefiboshet, and even the eulogy for Saul and Jonathan, indicate that the bitterness was very much alive.

We may now return to our original inquiry-why did David spare Saul? Once we have established that David did not have a pure loving and forgiving attitude towards Saul, it would appear that Ralbag and Abarbanell's assertion, that David was partially motivated by his own self-protection, has much merit.

But perhaps it is the opposite. From the Psalms and from David's references to Saul in the Book of Samuel, it is clear that David was tormented constantly by the king. David reacted as any normal individual would have-most likely with even greater intensity[15]-with animosity, exasperation, and even feelings of destructiveness. David confronted Saul possibly only hours after composing the most militant and malevolent of all his Psalms. Yet, he was able to transcend his potent emotions, and did not act on them. It is difficult to imagine that the mere desire to protect the institution of the monarchy would have played a significant role in stifling David's burning desire to eliminate Saul. It is far more plausible that David's immense piety intervened at those critical moments: how could he kill God's anointed, *meshi'ah Hashem?*[16]

In fact, many commentators explicate the superscription, *al tashhet* (see Psa. 57:1; 58:1; 59:1) in reference to the dual nature of David's prayer. Taking the phrase literally, meaning "do not destroy," some exegetes assert that David is praying for Saul not to destroy David (see Rashi 57:1), but others aver that David is praying that he not destroy Saul (see Alsheikh 57:1).[17] Rashi appears to combine these two approaches in his commentary to 57:2:

> "Have mercy on me, have mercy"-have mercy on me that I will not kill, and that I will not be killed..

This interpretation is consistent with Midrash Shoher Tov (Psalm 7:13):

> R. Yitzhak said, just as David prayed that he should not fall into the hands of Saul, so too he prayed that Saul should not fall into his hands.[18]

While the Psalms demonstrate David's hostility towards Saul, this conclusion serves only to enhance David's greatness and piety. David did not disregard life-threatening hostility directed at him; he was a real person with passionate human drives, one who wanted to lash out at his enemies. Our reading of the synthesized portrait of David from both Samuel and the Psalms shows a tormented, conflicted individual, one who passionately loved and resented his pursuer simultaneously.

In David's opportunities to kill Saul, always immediately following the composition of hostile Psalms, he was just barely able to control himself and his men. David, in his profound piety, recognized that Saul (as long as he was alive) was God's chosen one. David's staggering self-control, in the heat of such potent emotions, truly places him as one of the most exemplary righteous people in our history.

NOTES

1. All English translations of biblical verses are from The Jewish Publication Society Tanakh (Philadelphia: 1985), unless otherwise specified.

2. See also II Sam. 4:9-12, where David has Ish Boshet's assassins executed as well. See Abarbanel *ad loc.*

3. It is difficult to ascertain the exact chronological order of the composition of these Psalms, since some of the events referred to occurred more than once. For example, David hid in caves (Psalms 57, 142) both in I Sam. 22:1 and 24:3; he hid in the Wilderness of Judah (Psalm 63) in I Sam. 23:14; 23:24; 24:1; and 25:1. The Ziphites informed Saul of David's whereabouts (Psalm 54) in I Sam. 23:19 and 26:1. On several occasions, commentators attempt to pinpoint the specific events mentioned.

   See Berakhot 10a, which concludes that one cannot deduce anything from the juxtaposition of Psalms, since they clearly are assembled out of chronological sequence.

4. One might wish to add Psalms 34 and 60, which David composed in Philistia, while in flight from Saul.

5. See Amos Hakham (*Da'at Mikra*, Psalms, vol. I), pp. 15-18, for a fuller discussion on this topic.

6. On v. 6, Radak asserts a novel interpretation, that David is praying for the Day of Judgment in Messianic times. He avers that the entire verse does not fit into the general framework of the Psalm.

7. Malbim (Psa. 57:9) writes that Saul's pursuit of David hampered the latter's personality and soul. After Saul perished in battle, David's full personality was restored and burst forth

8. See I Sam. 17:43; 24:14; II Sam. 3:8; 9:8; 16:9; Ecc. 9:4.

9. Radak (v. 11) notes that the Hebrew literally reads, "may *he* (in the singular) be gutted by the sword, may *they* be prey for jackals." He explains that David first prays for Saul (his singular foe) to be killed by the sword (which in fact occurs in I Sam. 31), and then for Saul's men to be prey for jackals.

10. Rashi and Radak on this verse explain that this refers to David himself, who already was anointed (and therefore viewed himself as a king already). Radak adds that he perceived himself as fitting for the throne. CF. B.T. Megillah 14a-b.

11. Rashi (Psa. 18:1) writes that David composed this Psalm towards the end of his life. He specifies Saul because the king pursued David more than any other individual enemy. Ibn Ezra (Psa. 18:1) asserts that David wrote this Psalm after his men told him to remain home during battles, lest he be killed (II Sam. 22:17). With this view, Ibn Ezra can explain the position of the Psalm as it appears in II Sam. 22, immediately following the request of his men in the text.

12. See Rashi to Psa. 116:1, who maintains that that Psalm also was written by David out of relief when Saul was killed.

13. It is noteworthy that in Mo'ed Katan 16b, God castigates David for singing a hymn of glory at the downfall of the righteous Saul.

14. In fact, they often interpret many other general allusions to "enemies" in the Psalms as referring to Saul and his men. See, for example, Rashi Psa. 7:1,5; 11:1; 23:4.

15. See Sukkah 52a, where Abayyei states that the evil inclination of a Torah scholar is greater than that of the average individual. See also Lev. Rabbah 23:11; Ruth Rabbah 6:4, which compare David's restraint in his not killing Saul to that of Joseph's restraint in his avoiding an affair with Potiphar's wife.

16. The position of Ralbag and Abarbanel does seem in place, however, when David executes the Amalekite youth and Ish Boshet's assassins.

17. Malbim agrees with Alsheikh's interpretation of *al tashhet*, deriving its meaning from David's command to Abishai (I Sam. 26:9), *al tashhitehu* (don't do him violence).

18. See also Tanhuma *VaYishlah* 4, Rashi Gen. 32:8, where the Midrash explicates the apparent redundancy in Jacob's fear, "Then Jacob was greatly afraid and distressed." The Midrash explains, "Jacob was greatly afraid"-that he should not kill [Esau]; "and distressed"-that he [Jacob] should not be killed.

Similar to the David narrative, the simple reading of the text leads one to think that Jacob was concerned only about the safety of himself and his family. This Midrash points to a more righteous layer of anxiety, that Jacob did not want his passions to dictate his behavior to the extent that he might harm or kill his brother.

THE UNIVERSITY AND THE JEWISH STUDENT

by Norman Adler

I. INTRODUCTION

Like any other adolescent approaching college today, the Jewish student faces personal challenges. In particular, the Jewish student must resolve questions of how to maintain his or her cultural and religious identity in a setting (college) that may have values that differ from their home community. The main purpose of this essay is to describe some of the intellectual and personal conflicts the student must confront when entering college. I shall also outline the social and historical origins of these conflicts.

The first challenge comes from the sheer enormity of the task of choosing a college. Today, America offers over two thousand institutions of post-secondary education (with more than twelve million students enrolled). There are liberal arts colleges, graduate and research universities, technical schools, art institutes, music conservatories, religious seminaries, and a variety of vocational training schools from which the potential student may choose. Even at Yeshiva College, which prides itself on its small size, attention to every student, and its dual curriculum of liberal arts and classical Jewish studies, there are hundreds of course entries each year and over twenty majors

185

from which to choose.

Any student headed for college today must resolve numerous questions and conflicts. For Jewish students, these include how one becomes "educated" while remaining true to Torah values. In America, education and especially higher education, has traditionally provided ethnic groups access to the broader society and the chance to assume leadership positions therein. The cultural cost of entrance is sometimes high though - sometimes too high. It can lead to assimilation and loss of established ethnic and cultural values. At Yeshiva University, our educational goal is to furnish our young with the tools to survive and succeed in the increasingly multicultural world of the Diaspora - while maintaining their adherence to our tradition.

I take the following quotation from Amy Tan's novel *The Joy Luck Club*, which I find to be a poignant description of Chinese acculturation to America. The following passage, elegiac in tone, describes the sense of hope and loss common to the immigrant experience, including our own:

> The Old woman remembered a swan she had bought many years ago in Shanghai for a foolish sum. This bird, boasted the market vendor, was once a duck that stretched its neck in hopes of becoming a goose and now look!!! - it is too beautiful to eat.

Then the woman and the swan sailed across an ocean many thousands of li wide, stretching their necks toward America. On her journey she cooed to the swan: "In America I will have a daughter just like me. But over there nobody will say her worth is measured by the loudness of her husband's belch. Over there nobody will look down on her, because I will make her speak only perfect American English. And over there she will always be too full to swallow any sorrow! She will know my meaning, because I will give her this swan - a creature that became more than what was hoped for.

But when she arrived in the new country, the immigration officials pulled her swan away from her, leaving the woman fluttering her arms and with only one swan feather for a memory. And then she had to fill out so many forms she forgot why she had come and what she had left behind.

Now the woman was old. And she had a daughter who grew up speaking only English and swallowing more Coca-Cola than sorrow. For a long time now the woman had wanted to give her daughter the single swan feather and tell her, 'This feather may look worthless, but it comes from afar and carries with it all my good intentions.' And she waited, year after year, for the day she could tell her daughter this in perfect American English."[1]

If we substitute our traditional Jewish values in place of Chinese values, the passage is more than poignant for us. It becomes tragic - because the forcible removal of the "swan" (representing ancient tradition) symbolizes the loss of core values. We are thus faced with the problem of how to give our children a modern secular education while strengthening their connection to Torah. The culture conflict reflects the origins of the modern college.

II. ORIGINS OF THE UNIVERSITY

One of the reasons that the values of the university may not be totally congruent with those of traditional Judaism is that the academy has a long history and is derived from a variety of cultural sources. The university, with its intellectual foundation in the academies of Plato and Aristotle, was committed to the ideals of rationalism (and empiricism). If we, as Jews, constantly look to Jerusalem, the professoriate faces Athens, with its idealization of the mind.

Structurally, the modern university is medieval in origin. Students in the medieval university were all men - aristocratic and Christian. They studied seven subjects: grammar, rhetoric, logic, arithmetic, geometry, music, and astronomy - the trivium and the quadrivium (the first part metaphysically related to the trinity of the Church, which was the foundation of the university). The modern descendant of this Classical Core education is the liberal arts curriculum that most students are required to take before concentrating on a major.

The "major" as an intellectual entity came into existence during the next major stage of academic evolution: the German University of the 19th century. This institution added scientific and technical investigation to the classical core of its medieval progenitor. Systematic analyses were emphasized, and students became "intellectual apprentices" in the larger purpose of "knowledge production". Their modern descendants are perhaps the graduate students working around the clock in scientific laboratories.[2]

The present day university is very much influenced by American pedagogy, especially pedagogical thinking of the quintessential American, Benjamin Franklin. Franklin believed that education should be "practical" - by this he did not mean crassly vocational or utilitarian but "practical" in the sense of integrated with society and with life. Instead of treating the academy as a walled institution separated from the medieval town, Franklin combined classical with modern utilitarian knowledge. Science and technology now took their place with arts and letters.

Consequentially, education came to include professional and career training, a trend accelerated by the development of state (public) universities. *Formally*, the modern university is the descendent of all these institutions. Combining graduate training, research, government and public service, training for future jobs - universities are sometimes a bewildering place for the young college student, especially one trying to adhere to his or her religious tradition.

III. THE NATURE OF THE STUDENT

Like any other culture, the university depends on the interaction of the institutional structure with its members (students). To the extent that the institution "expects" certain patterns from its members, another challenge is college expectations of its students. William Perry made a study of the psychological development of the college student[3]. At the first stage, the student looks for the "correct answers" to a problem. Then, students progress to a stage where they look for the relativistic context in which the answer is to be placed. An answer may be right "depending on how one looks at it". Finally, there is a stage of "committed relativism" in which students find their bearing - but do so in a world of multiple values.

While Perry's study was supposed to be descriptive, it probably represents the values that most university professors would accept as correct. For those of us who want students to become educated but to retain their Jewish identity and practice, these values may be somewhat problematical. The Perry model is not necessarily that of the Talmid Haham, though it is not necessarily incompatible with it either.

IV. CULTURES ON CAMPUS

Most schools with large Jewish populations have at least a few resources to accommodate these student's religious and cultural needs. Hillel Foundations, Lubavitch Houses, local synagogues and Jewish role models on the faculty all provide means for the students to express their Jewishness. Given the rate of Jewish intermarriage (and a wide variety of other social indexes of the state of American Jewry), these resources have not proven sufficient for the maintenance of an intellectually elite Jewish intelligentsia that is at the same time committed to core Jewish values.

A bolder experiment was the development of a truly "Jewish University", Yeshiva College. Formed during the 1920's, Yeshiva College was the first Jewish university to be born in the Diaspora. Yeshiva College was specifically set up to accommodate secular learning while developing a student's Jewish background. In my opinion, it is still the pre-eminent institution of its type. Having adopted a formal "Yeshiva/collegiate" model, we can be fully committed to both sacred and secular knowledge *(Torah U-Madda)*. Formally, our students are rigorously trained in the classical texts of Judaism and the most modern of liberal arts, sciences, business, and pre-professional studies.

There are other academic/Jewish models today, e.g. Bar-Ilan, Touro, and Brandeis. These are less intensively committed to *Torah U-Madda*. Inevitably, culture conflicts can occur. Recall the difficulty Brandeis had a few years ago when, as a secular university with Jewish consciousness, it came under pressure to serve non-Kosher food "overtly".[4]

On campuses across the country, multiculturalism has

caused strains between campus constituencies. The growth of ethnic studies, ebonics, women's studies, and Jewish studies - put divergent pressures for common resources. This is part of the normal academic process of governance. Sometimes, however, cultural conflict spills over into the life of the campus, pitting one group against the other.

From the point of view of the typical American university, it is of course difficult to reconcile all of the competing requests. When faced with writing a "complete" history of California that would be acceptable for adoption in its schools, the project editor had to say:

> My response was, you can't produce a book which is all-inclusive. You can't emphasize the Chinese in San Francisco and the Armenians in Fresno and the Portuguese in San Pablo, and the Italians in North Beach and the Koreans in LA. You can't write the history of every ethnic group in California. You certainly can't do it for the entire country.[5]

All of this is not to say that a student cannot function Jewishly on the American campus. By remaining true to his or her religious heritage, it is certainly possible to grow. While remaining true to Torah values, the student must learn to co-exist with, if not fully accept, the dominant mores of the college culture (and by extension the larger society). These "western" values today include democratic values, tolerance for dissent, critical analysis, and multiculturalism (at least in the narrower sense of appreciation for a variety of points of view). The core values we expect of the Jewish student religiously are *Yirat Shamayim*, organic connection to our tradition, and observance.

The Jewish and secular systems converge on two points:

1. The need for analysis and the use of the mind to discover the intricacies of the system.
2. The acquisition of an outlook that leads to the "good life".

For the western philosophical tradition, this is the "examined life". For the religious, it is the observant one.

V. CONCLUSIONS

There is a value judgment in all that I have written here. It is important for an American Jewish student to acquire a college education today. It is important because philosophically I believe that the life of the mind is a critical human activity and that our tradition encourages this activity.

There is a second, more practical reason too. An education is important because society is becoming increasingly technical. According to the bureau of labor statistics, the highest growth professions in the next decade will continue to be the service professions - paramedical, computer based, and technical. These cannot be acquired by apprenticeship, as in the old days. A university degree is necessary, if not always sufficient, for most students to earn a good living, support a family, and educate their children Jewishly.

Of course, I believe the model developed by my school, Yeshiva University, is the most functional for educating the Jewish student. Our dual curriculum is the embodiment of *Torah U-Madda* (Jewish and secular knowledge)[6]. Other, less intensively Jewish institutions also offer opportunities for the Jewish student to acquire a modern education that will enable him or her to enter the work force and to be an educated human being.

Whatever school an individual student enters, however, it

is important to consider the synergies and conflicts involved in becoming an educated Jew. It was the purpose of this essay to outline some of the dimensions this thought requires and to emphasize its importance. I close with a quotation from Dr. Norman Lamm's book *Torah U-Madda*:

> the aspirations of *Torah Umadda* are thought by him to vindicate the faith that the encounter between the two can be fully creative. ....
>
> *Torah* and *Madda* are fundamentally compatible; perhaps, in an ultimate sense they can be said to have once constituted a unity. Hence in seeking to bring the two together, we are not endeavoring to combine two disparate entities de novo.[7]

NOTES

1. Amy Tan, *The Joy Luck Club*, (New York: Ballantine, 1989), pp. 3-4.

2. One of the problems prominently discussed in the press today is that undergraduates (and their parents who pay for their education) are not the central concern of the large research universities.

3. Perry, William, *Forms of Intellectual and Ethical Development in the College Years*, (New York: Holt, 1970).

4. It was not so much the serving of the food as the symbolism of doing so in a "Jewish" institution that caused uproar.

5. Gary Nash, quoted in Gitlin, Todd. *The Twilight of Common Dreams*, (New York: Holt, 1995), p. 19.

6. Norman Lamm, *Torah U-Madda*, (New Jersey: Jason Aronson, 1990). The concept might also apply to S. R. Hirsch's *Torah im Derekh Eretz* (though this could be argued).

7. Lamm, 139.

ABOUT THE CONTRIBUTORS

Dr. Norman Adler is Dean of Yeshiva College.

Rabbi Hayyim Angel is Assistant Rabbi of Congregation Shearith Israel and teaches Bible at Yeshiva College.

Dr. Marc D. Angel is Rabbi of Congregation Shearith Israel, and has written and edited seventeen books.

Ronda Angel Arking is an editor and writer.

Dr. Reuven Bulka is Rabbi of Congregation Machzikei Hadas in Ottawa, and is the author of numerous books relating to Judaism and psychology.

Fortuna Calvo-Roth is president of Coral Communications Group, LLC and partner of Vista magazine.

Dr. Louis H. Feldman is Professor of Classics at Yeshiva University, and has published extensively on the history of Jews in classical antiquity.

Dr. Jeffrey Gurock is the Libby M. Klapperman Professor of Jewish History at Yeshiva University.

Rabbi Howard Joseph is Rabbi of Congregation Shearith Israel, the Spanish and Portuguese Synagogue of Montreal.

Judge Judith S. Kaye is Chief Judge of the State of New York.

Dr. Menachem Kellner is Wolfson Professor of Jewish Thought at the University of Haifa.

Dr. Walter S. Wurzburger is Rabbi Emeritus of Congregation Shaaray Tefila in Lawrence, New York, and for many years served as editor of the quarterly journal *Tradition*. He has published extensively in the fields of Jewish philosophy and ethics.